'It worked for me'

VICKI LANSKY

Illustrations by David Lock

EXLEY

Published in Great Britain in 1985
by Exley Publications Ltd,
16 Chalk Hill, Watford, Herts WD1 4BN, United Kingdom.
Second printing 1986
Third printing 1988
Fourth printing 1989

First published in 1980 in the USA.

British Library Cataloguing in Publication Data
Lansky, Vicki.
It worked for me. [1001 practical tips for parents]
1. Child rearing.
I. [1001 practical tips for parents].
II. Title.
649'.1 HQ769

ISBN 1-85015-027-3 (Hbk)
ISBN 1-85015-076-1 (Pbk)

Illustrations by David Lock.
Typeset by Brush Off Studios, St Albans, Herts.
Printed and bound in Hungary.

Introduction

My first child had the good grace to arrive at the end of May, so I was able to wheel him to the park almost daily. For him there was the fresh air and sunshine — for me there were the other new mothers on the park bench. It did not take me long to discover that their babies too revised their waking hours nightly and were grizzly in the evenings when adults longed for private time. To my relief I found I didn't have the only child who hadn't read Dr. Spock!

Not only did I get support from these park bench mothers — I got a lot of ideas from them. These weren't the kind of ideas I read in babycare books or heard in the baby clinic. They were practical tips born of experience, so they seemed worth trying. Other mothers, I was finding, were a wonderful source of information.

In 1979 I began publishing a newsletter called Practical Parenting *because I still wanted to know more about what was working for other parents. Each issue of the newsletter includes a place for readers to answer questions asked by other parents. We ask parents to share their questions, recipes, tips and experiences. So from the tips sent in to the newsletter, from word of mouth ('the mothers' network'), from my experiences, from sources of all kinds, I have collected the best of childcare tips that parents have shared for the first five years of living with small children.*

Contents

1. New Baby Care

2. Child Care: the Basics

3. Hygiene and Health

4. Coping with Children at Home

5. The Challenge of Parenting

6. *Family Heritage*

7. *Families on the Go*

8. Child's Play

9. Special Situations

Chapter One

New Baby Care

Having a baby is not unlike entering a tunnel. We can't see the end and we wonder what we have got ourselves into! We emerge five years later, having had less sleep than we might have wished, but thinking that it wasn't so bad, after all. The difficult days become difficult to remember.

Despite the newness of everything we must do, it doesn't really take long to become old hands at baby care. Though babies don't arrive with attached instructions, they do express their needs loud and clear. And as far as our expertize is concerned, new babies don't realize that everything we do first time round is just as new for us as it is for them . . . WHEW!

YOUR NEW BABY AND YOU

Amid the excitement that follows the birth of a baby, it's important to remember that everyone has adjustments to make. If it's your first child, 'Mum' and 'Dad' are new roles to be tried out. If there are siblings in the house, their positions in the family are changed — overnight.

Along with the excitement and pride that follow a birth come stress and fatigue. We're apt to demand more of ourselves than we do of those around us, but taking care of yourself adequately will make you more able to help everybody else cope with the adjustments. It's time for spouses to be good to each other and to put off big decisions, if possible.

- Find a 'Do Not Disturb' sign and put it on your front door. Or make a sign: 'Ssssh! Baby and Mummy are resting!'
- If you don't want to answer the phone, leave the receiver off, or, if you can, turn the volume control right down so you can't hear it ringing. If you have one of the new socket-type installations, you can unplug it at the socket and this will stop the phone ringing.
- Let modern technology help you avoid answering the phone when you don't want to. Record the details of your baby's birth on a telephone answering machine and add a message about when would be the best time to call.
- Make some part of every day special, for spouses only, whether it's a late dinner together, going out for a walk or just a five-minute lunch-time telephone call.
- *Get out*, alone or as a couple, on a regular basis.
- Don't worry if you don't feel overwhelming love for your infant instantly. It often takes some time, maybe months, for real parental love to develop. Relax and enjoy the developing bond between you and your baby.
- Find some support, either a friend who also has a new baby or an organized group.

FEEDING YOUR BABY

A baby's stomach is about the size of its fist — taking in a lot of milk at one time just isn't possible. No wonder infants spend so much time eating!

If you're breastfeeding, the first rule is to relax. Find a quiet place, away from distractions and visitors, for your first feeds. And don't watch the clock — the baby doesn't. If the father feels a bit left out, remember that there are things he can do, such as changing and bathing the baby and bringing it to your bed for night feeds. Some parents decide to give the baby one bottle of formula a day, both to help involve Dad and to let Mum get some sleep or to give her a chance to get out of the house. If you use powdered infant formula, it's easy to make just one bottle at a time.

Support for the Nursing Mother
The National Childbirth Trust has 504 breastfeeding counsellors who are trained to help and support mothers with breastfeeding. To find out about the work of the National Childbirth Trust and your nearest representative, contact them at Alexandra House, Oldham Terrace, Acton, London W3 6NH. Telephone: 01-992 8637.

Dressing comfortably for breastfeeding

- Take a front-buttoning nightdress or one with concealed slits with you to hospital.
- Wear a stretch bra, if you like, which can simply be lifted up for nursing. Some women buy bras before they go to hospital, getting a size larger (and a *cup* size larger) than they wore during pregnancy, but this isn't right for everyone. . . . Perhaps it would be best just to cut the sides of your bra and insert pieces of elastic if you do need some extra 'give'.

- Try using a man's soft handkerchief in your bra cup to prevents leaks from coming through, or use about four layers of an old knitted vest or stitch together two- to three-inch circles of towelling and use these. Or cut a sanitary towel or nappy to fit. (And of course there are commercially available nursing pads or other products.)
- Remember that printed tops will make stains less visible if you do leak.
- Unbutton front-buttoning blouses from the bottom for modest nursing. Or wear a knitted jumper; the baby's head will cover your bare midriff, and the jumper will cover your breast.
- Keep a loose-fitting cardigan handy and don't overlook the quick cover-up possibilities of ponchos, scarves or baby blankets or shawls.

Nursing techniques

- Protect sheets and blankets, when you nurse in bed, by covering them with a cot-sized waterproof sheet.
- Use a large pillow for nursing in bed.
- Wrap yourself and the baby in a big blanket in the winter if you sit up to nurse at night. Milk flows better if you're warm and cosy.
- Choose a cushioned rocking chair, armchair or sofa for nursing when you're up, one with low arms to rest your own arms on, and put a pillow under your nursing arm. If you're buying a rocking chair, remember that a wooden one will be easier to keep clean than an upholstered one.
- Put the baby on a pillow on your lap; you find that doing so puts him or her at just the right level for comfort.
- Keep track of which breast you used last by transferring a safety pin from one bra strap to the other. Or buy a lightweight expandable bracelet and slip it from one wrist to the other. Or use a ring that is loose enough to transfer easily from hand to hand. You may want to start on the right side each morning; you'll be able to remember how many times you've fed the baby and work it out. Most mothers start nursing with the breast used *last*.

- Put your finger in the corner of the baby's mouth to break the suction and ease him or her off your breast, when you want to stop nursing.
- If the baby falls asleep, a nappy-change will help to wake him or her up when you're ready to change breasts.
- Wear a bright 'necklace' of coloured wooden beads or ribbons for your baby to look at while you're nursing.
- Remember that some babies find it hard to settle down against slippery nylon or polyester. If you're wearing a blouse or top of either fabric, slip a nappy or small blanket between yourself and the baby.
- Try expressing milk in a warm shower or bath if you're engorged and the baby isn't ready to nurse. Experiment with various types of breast pumps; they don't all work for everyone.

Bottle-feeding

It's understood today that a baby's food needn't be really warm, but it goes against the grain for some parents to give a cold bottle. A fancy electric bottle warmer isn't necessary, though. Take the chill off in any way you wish, and use the time while the bottle's heating to change the baby. Test the temperature of the formula by squirting a drop onto your wrist; if it feels comfortably warm, it's all right for the baby.

While it isn't critical for development, some parents hold their babies in one arm for one feed, the other for the next, to help the infants develop a good eye muscle coordination.

- Warm a bottle by standing it in a couple of inches of water in an electric kettle for a few minutes, by putting it in any handy bowl, pan or mug of hot water or by running hot tap water over it. Shake the bottle occasionally to warm the formula evenly.
- Stand an uncapped eight-ounce bottle in your microwave at high power for 15 to 30 seconds if it's at room temperature and for 30 to 60 seconds if it's straight from the refrigerator.
- Keep extra formula in the refrigerator to add to a bottle that's too warm.

- Make middle-of-the-night feeds easier by taking a *cold* (from the refrigerator) bottle to your room or the baby's when you go to bed. It will probably warm to room temperature by the time you need it.
- Regulate the flow by loosening the bottle collar if the flow is too slow, tightening it if the flow is too fast.
- Hold the bottle at feeding angle to check the teat hole size. If the formula comes out in steady, even drops, the teat is ready for use.

The business of bottles

- Store bottles in the refrigerator in an empty ice cream container to keep them together and to stop them tipping over. Or make and store formula in a sterilized glass coffee pot or measuring jug with lid.
- Boil teats in water in a glass jar in the microwave oven to clean them. A teaspoonful of vinegar in the water will prevent hard water deposits forming on the jar.
- Enlarge teat holes, if necessary, by putting toothpicks in them and boiling the teats for three minutes, or by sticking a very hot needle into the rubber a few times. If the hole is too big, throw the teat away and start using the spare ones you bought.
- Rinse out empty bottles as soon as possible or you'll find 'cottage cheese' in them later. Shake a bottle filled with warm water and dry rice to remove the milk rings. To get rid of a sour-milk smell, fill bottles with warm water, add a teaspoon of baking soda, shake well and leave them to stand overnight.
- Remove juice stains by putting baking soda and warm water in the bottle and scrubbing with a bottle brush. If juice pulp blocks the teat, cover the top of the bottle with a piece of muslin and strain the juice through it.
- Wash bottles in the dishwasher, if you have one. They won't need sterilizing.

Burping

Don't worry if your baby doesn't always burp after a feed, especially if you're breastfeeding. If he or she seems comfortable

after you've had a good try, leave it. Do be careful not to 'pat' too hard; you may cause the baby to vomit. Some parents find it better to use a gentle upward stroke instead of patting.

- Put your baby on your shoulder with a nappy underneath and gently pat his or her back between the shoulder blades.
- Tie a bib around *your* neck if you get tired of using a nappy, and switch the bib from shoulder to shoulder as you switch the baby.
- Lay the baby on your lap, tummy down, with his or her head turned a little to the side. Pat or gently rub, from the bottom up.
- Make a 'horseshoe' with your thumb and index finger and put the baby's chin into it whilst he or she sits on your lap, leaning against your arm. Pat or stroke upwards.
- Put your hand under the baby's breastbone and lean the baby towards your palm (covered with a cloth or nappy), while firmly but gently rubbing his or her back.
- Squeeze the baby's back gently, while the baby is on your shoulder or in your lap, beginning at the kidney area and working slowly up to the shoulders.

PUTTING YOUR BABY TO SLEEP

Some babies sleep for long stretches at a time, others catnap and many seem to prefer sleeping during the day rather than at night. A new baby sleeping through the night is the exception, not the rule, whatever your friends and relatives may say. During the first three to six months, parents usually have to adjust their own sleeping habits to the baby's, or take it in turns, to avoid exhaustion. (And, in fact, one definition of a parent is 'a person who is no longer *ever* guaranteed a full night's sleep.')

Inducing sleep

Sometimes babies need a little time to cry or fuss before sleeping. You'll soon know if the crying means something serious. Your first thought will be for the baby's comfort. Position him or her on the side or stomach first — some people say sleeping on the back is best avoided to prevent newborn babies from choking on milk they may bring up.

It's not necessary or practical to try to live in a silent house. If you maintain a reasonable level of noise, the baby will get used to it. You may wish to play a radio softly just outside the baby's room. (But if you find that the shrill ring of the phone does wake the baby, put a mat under the phone; a thick pot-holder works nicely.) Remember that giving the baby a feeling of security is the most important thing.

- Establish a 'sleep routine' from the beginning, especially if you'll be travelling or expecting the baby to sleep in different places. Sing the same lullaby every time and rub a special spot, perhaps the back of the head or the forehead, and rub that spot at sleeping time *only*.
- Attach springs to the bottoms of the cot legs and try rocking the baby to sleep.
- Spray the cot sheets very lightly with the same perfume you used in the hospital and it will seem to your baby that you are near.
- Try confining the baby gently, wrapping him or her lightly in a blanket. Some babies sleep better with a rather firm swaddling, reminiscent of the pre-birth environment.
- Place the baby on his or her side. Roll up two cot blankets and put one roll behind the baby's back, the other in front of the stomach. Tuck in snugly.

- Position the baby in a corner of the crib or cot with his or her head touching the bumper or soft padding to provide a feeling of security. This also allows you to move the baby from corner to corner if the sheet gets wet or soiled.
- Let the baby sleep upright occasionally, if he or she prefers it, using an infant seat or carrying him or her in a soft fabric baby carrier.
- Slip a warm heating pad or hot water bottle onto the sheet when you take the baby out for a feed so that the bed will be warm when you return him or her to it (but then take the pad or bottle out). Or warm a blanket in the tumble dryer, if you have one, while you feed the baby.
- Tape record the sound of running water and play it to lull a child to sleep. The sound of running water simulates intra-uterine sounds.

When the baby confuses day and night

This phenomenon is often associated with colic. If the father goes to work and the mother stays at home, it's logical that she bears the brunt, but she must catch up on her sleep during the day, when the baby is asleep. If both work, they must share the night-time discomfort.

- Try to keep the baby awake during the early evening to encourage the swing to night-time sleeping. Keep the baby slightly cool and upright in an infant seat or carrier. Talk, sing, dance or do whatever will stimulate the baby.
- Add a little cereal to the last evening bottle for a more substantial meal.
- Change bathtime to just before bedtime so the baby will be relaxed.
- Give night feeds in dim light so the baby will realize that they're different from daytime feeds.
- Avoid too many visitors and too much handling of the baby by strangers, which can overstimulate the baby and make sleeping difficult.
- Allow yourself a good cry. This, too, will pass.

Making night checking easier

- Put a dimmer on the light switch.
- Keep a soft night-light burning in the baby's room.
- Use a torch; keep it near your bed.
- Apply petroleum jelly or vegetable oil to the side rails of the cot to stop them squeaking when they're raised or lowered. Or rub them with waxed paper.

Keeping your baby cosy

- By gently touching the back of the baby's neck you can find out if he or she is comfortable. (Make sure your hand is not cold; warm it next to your body or under hot water first if necessary.) If the baby's neck is warm, he or she is comfortable. If it's damp, the baby may be too warm. Arms and legs can also give you an idea if the baby is comfortable, and you should look for a pink or rosy colour. Don't go by feeling the baby's hands — they usually feel cool.
- Use sleeping suits of various thicknesses, depending on the time of year, and, if necessary, leave off a blanket altogether. If you're really worried about the baby being cold, put on two sleeping suits, but make sure they are not too tight otherwise the baby's circulation might get cut off.
- Use a small PVC sheet with terry towel facing over the bottom cot sheet, or spread a nappy over it, so that you don't have to change the big sheet every time it's soiled and disturb the baby.

WHEN YOUR BABY CRIES

Babies cry and fuss for a variety of reasons, but you'll soon be able to recognize the cry of distress. Obvious solutions are available for many cries, including those of discomfort from being too cool or too warm, simple boredom or relief of tension. The first thing parents usually look for is a nappy pin that has come undone; another is for a tiny thread on the inside of a garment (or even a thread from the sheets or blankets) that has got tangled round the baby's hand or foot and is hurting. Experienced parents check carefully and cut all loose threads off.

Sometimes, a baby just cries . . . and cries . . . and cries . . . and you know there's nothing wrong, no physical reason for it. Don't feel guilty — the baby isn't crying because you're a 'bad' parent — there's nothing personal in it.

20 Ways to Cope with Crying

1. Walk or dance with the baby. Try dancing to different kinds of music.
2. Rock the baby.
3. Bounce the baby gently in your arms or on a bed. A water bed is especially soothing.
4. Take the baby for a ride in the pram or the car.
5. Put the baby in a wind-up swing.
6. Turn up the music on the radio or stereo, put on the vacuum cleaner or a hair dryer.
7. Offer the baby a 'noisy' toy; shake it, rattle it.
8. Sing or talk to the baby in a quiet, sing-song way.
9. Carry the baby with you round the house in a baby carrier, close to your body.
10. Lay the baby tummy down across your lap and gently rub his or her back.
11. Lay the baby across a warm hot-water bottle on your lap or a bed.
12. Massage the baby's body and limbs gently; use a warmed lotion, if the weather is cool.
13. Wrap the baby up tightly.
14. Feed and burp the baby again. Or offer a little warm water. In desperation, add a little sugar to the water or to weak camomile tea.
15. Offer a dummy and hold it in the baby's mouth if necessary.
16. Or let the baby suck the top of your little finger (turning your nail down so it won't poke the roof of the baby's mouth if he or she sucks hard).
17. Hold the baby close and breathe slowly and calmly; the baby may feel your calmness and become quiet.
18. Cross the baby's arms across the chest and hold him or her down on a bed with a gentle, firm pressure.
19. Let someone else take over while you go out. If one of the family is not available, ask a neighbour or friend if they can baby-sit for you.
20. If *nothing* works, put the baby in his or her bed, close the door and turn up the TV or radio. Take a shower to drown the noise and to relax yourself. Take a look at the child every 15 minutes or so, for your own peace of mind.

Colic

Colic is not a disease; it can't be tested for. It's a symptom of severe cramp in the digestive tract. The baby pulls the legs up, clenches the fists and the face turns bright red. Crying may go on for hours, often in the late afternoon and evening. Fortunately, colic rarely lasts past the third month of a child's life, but until it's over, it's hard on both baby and parents.

In a breastfed baby, colic may be caused by a reaction to something in the mother's diet. She may try avoiding such things as strong-flavoured foods and drinks that contain caffeine. A recent discovery is that some babies are allergic to milk and other dairy products that their mothers drink or eat. A change to a soya formula that does not contain corn syrup or corn solids often helps colicky babies, too. Consult your doctor before you make a change.

- Try to handle and feed the baby calmly. A parent's tension may be transmitted to the baby and cause stress that brings on colic.
- Try burping the baby *before* starting a feed to prevent a bubble from being trapped at the bottom of the stomach. And burp the baby several times during a feed.
- Feed the baby in as nearly an upright position as possible. The bubble at the bottom of the baby's stomach will rise towards the top of the food and be burped easily, preventing the pain caused by trapped wind.
- Mix equal amounts of 7-Up and water in a three-ounce bottle and give it to a colicky baby between feeds to help him or her pass wind.
- Or lay the baby in the cot on his or her back, pull the left arm and right leg gently, then the right arm and the left leg, to relieve wind.
- If it becomes really trying, see your doctor as he may be able to prescribe a medicine.

KEEPING YOUR BABY CLEAN

You won't be giving your baby a full bath until the umbilical cord falls off. Even then, remember that babies don't really get dirty, except for their bottoms, faces and necks. First babies probably get bathed more than others, simply because parents have more time than they do with two or more children. A day without a bath is *not* a disgrace; skipping a day, or even several days, may be best for both you and the baby. On the other hand, when you both feel the need of relaxation, a long warm bath together may help. You'll soon learn the best time of day for baths; immediately after a meal is best for some, but not for everyone.

Try not to be nervous when you bath your baby the first few times. Relax and enjoy it, and it will soon become routine. Make sure everything you need is within reach before starting, and try using only a little water in the bath until you become confident.

Bath equipment

- Make do at first with a plastic washing-up bowl on the kitchen work surface.
- Bath a new-born baby in a baby bath with a sloped back and headrest.
- Or bath the baby in the bathroom or kitchen sink, as long as he or she is not likely to bump into the taps. Be careful when the baby begins to kick as his or her head may get bumped against the side of the sink.
- Clip a large towel around your own neck, like a bib. It will keep you dry during the bath and give you an instant robe for the baby.

Bathing routines

- Run the cold water to the sink last if you have a mixer tap so that if the baby touches the tap it won't be hot and burn him or her.
- Use even mild baby soap sparingly to preserve the baby's own protective skin oils; soap is often responsible for skin rashes.
- Put a smear of cold cream or petroleum jelly on the baby's brows to channel soap away from his or her eyes.
- Put the plastic bottle of lotion or shampoo in the bath with the baby and it will be warm when you're ready to use it.
- Prevent cradle cap by combing even a bald head daily. Shampoo often and use a soft bristle brush or soft toothbrush (the long handle provides good manoeuverability).
- Treat cradle cap by smearing on baby oil or petroleum jelly at night and washing it off in the morning with a soapy flannel. Or try a paste of baking soda and water.
- Put any powder you use into your hand first, away from the baby's face, so that powder in the air isn't inhaled by the baby. And for the same reason, don't let an older baby play with an open powder container.

Preventing nappy rash

Experienced parents may smile a bit at the thought of 'preventing' nappy rash. It seems that almost every baby has it, to some degree, at one time or another.

- Give the baby warm, soapy baths, with mild soap.
- Mix baby powder in equal amounts with cornflour to save money and still have the smell of fresh baby powder plus extra protection from wetness.
- Don't use plastic pants, which hold moisture in — be prepared to change the baby often and to accumulate a lot of washing.
- Consider using disposable nappies, if you've been using cloth ones. Some, but not all babies who wear disposable nappies seem less likely to have nappy rash.

- Don't use fabric conditioner with every nappy wash. Babies are often sensitive to a build-up of conditioner (and over-use makes nappies less absorbent).

Treating nappy rash

Once the baby has nappy rash, you try one thing . . . and then another. Many doctors oppose greasing a baby with oil and lotions, and experienced parents don't use any solutions or ointments too thickly — 'more is better' doesn't apply here.

- Smooth on vegetable fat; it's cheaper than commercial preparations and usually works just as well. Petroleum jelly, which costs about the same, is also good.
- Or 'toast' ordinary flour in the oven and smooth it on the rash.
- Try applying zinc oxide or a paste of cornflour and water. (Current opinion is mixed as to the advisability of using cornflour alone, however.)
- Let the baby stay naked or at least bare-bottomed as often as possible — a slight case of nappy rash may be air/sun-cured quickly.
- Dry the baby's bottom with a hair dryer on a warm setting and held at least six inches from the skin.

- You may find an over-the-counter preparation that works. If serious nappy rash persists, get advice from your doctor or health visitor.

NAPPIES

Don't worry if you've never changed a nappy before. Mothers quickly become expert and not only *can* but *do* change nappies in their sleep — fathers, too. Disposable nappies are the easiest to use, and you can save money by buying in bulk. Whatever you decide to use, disposable nappies are ideal for the first few weeks, when you need to save your energy. Terry nappies are cheaper in the long run and are ecologically more acceptable to some people.

Cleaning bottoms

Some parents like the convenience of pre-moistened towelettes for cleaning babies' bottoms, but there are lots of alternatives.

- Make your own inexpensive wipes by thoroughly soaking a roll of toilet tissue (the strong kind — not extra soft) in baby oil in a shallow bowl. Pull out the centre core and start the roll from the middle. Store in a plastic bag or covered container.
- Keep a roll of toilet paper or a box of tissues where you change the baby for cleaning up.
- Or try torn-up old terry nappies, which you can wash with the other nappies.
- Clean a soiled bottom with oil on a cotton wool ball.

- Colour code flannels, if you use them for cleaning up: one colour for the bath, one for nappy changes.

Changing nappies

- Fold the plastic top of a disposable nappy down to the inside to prevent the wetness soaking into other clothing.
- Keep a roll of masking tape handy to mend torn tabs on disposable nappies and to mend plastic pants.
- Try using disposable nappies with elastic around the legs to prevent leaks. Tiny babies' legs aren't big enough to allow for a snug fit.
- Cover a baby boy's penis with your hand or a cloth as you expose it, to avoid being squirted. Point it down when you fasten the nappy to head the stream where you want it.
- Cut what you need from a roll of gauze to cover a circumcision. The roll is less expensive than pre-cut squares and works as well if not better.

Nappy pins

Nappy pins with plastic-covered ends are what you need — not ordinary safety pins. Always place your fingers between the baby's skin and the nappy so you don't stick the pin into the baby.

- Attach a wrist pincushion to the top of the cot or to the baby's changing table to use as a nappy pin holder when the baby is tiny. It's not safe to do this when the baby is old enough to reach for it. Otherwise stick the pins into a thick pot-holder or hang closed pins on a cup hook screwed into the wall.
- To get pins to slide through cloth easily, stick them into a bar of soap. Leave the wrapping on to stop any flakes falling out. Or, for an attractive pin holder, stick them into a decorative candle.
- Run pins through a strand of your hair or across the top of your head to make them go through cloth easily.
- Attach a few nappy pins to your keyring so that you'll always have some spare ones with you when you're out.
- Don't *ever* hold pins in your mouth — babies are great imitators.

Making the changing area convenient

You may find it practical to set up a second changing area to save your feet. Keep it stocked with nappies, clothing and duplicates of other essential items. Try to make the main changing area light and bright, but consider installing a dimmer switch for night-time changing.

- Use the top of a chest of drawers for a changing table. Cut an old belt in half and staple the ends to the top of it to make a safety belt for the baby. Line the drawers with wrapping paper from your baby gifts to make them attractive.
- Cover your changing mat with a pillowcase, which can be removed and washed easily.
- Put a shelf above the changing table to hold necessities and to keep them out of reach of toddlers in the house.
- Or make or buy a wall hanger (about two feet square) with pockets to fit small articles into. It can be hung with curtain rods at the top and bottom.
- Keep a thermos of warm water near the changing table at night for quick clean-ups. You'll avoid stumbling around in the dark and running the water for what seems hours to get the right temperature.
- Save time by folding nappies only as you need them. Keep a laundry basket of clean, unfolded nappies near the changing area.
- Have two nappy pails: a smallish one for soiled nappies (if you use terry nappies, half fill the bucket with water and add borax to stop it getting smelly) and one for wet or soiled clothing that's waiting to be washed.
- Cut down on cleaning by using plastic liners inside the nappy pail.

BABY LAUNDRY

It's unbelievable to new parents that one tiny person can generate so much washing — and it's always a surprise, even to those who have gone through it more than once. If you use terry nappies, you need them not only clean but also germ-free, to help prevent nappy rash.

Nappies

- Rinse out nappies, even those that are only wet, before putting them in the nappy pail. Empty soiled nappies in the toilet.
- Sprinkle a little baking soda in the nappy pail to stop the nappies smelling nasty.
- Soak nappies overnight in a sanitising powder and rinse them thoroughly the next day. If you want to wash them as well, do them on the normal programme and to make sure they are thoroughly rinsed go through the programme again without using washing powder.
- Or soak in a plastic bag in the nappy pail with water to which about a cup of borax has been added.
- If you're rinsing by hand, add a handful of baking soda to the next-to-last rinse to keep the nappies soft and smelling fresh. Fabric conditioner is expensive and may irritate the baby's skin.
- Or, again if you're doing them by hand, try another old-fashioned nappy softener and whitener — vinegar. A cupful in the second rinse gets rid of soap, too, and helps prevent nappy rash.

Plastic pants

- Dry plastic pants on a trouser hanger to avoid the heat of a tumble dryer. Hang them in the sun to kill any smells.
- Or dry them in the tumble dryer, but use a conditioner or put a few towels in as well.
- Rub a little baby oil into plastic pants that are becoming dry and brittle. Or try putting the oil into the rinsing water.

Stained clothes

- Soak stained clothes (or mildewed hand-me-downs) in hot water with half a cup each of vinegar and washing powder.
- Or soak overnight in hot water with a cupful each of washing powder, bleach and dishwasher powder. In the morning, run the clothes through the normal warm wash programme and give them an extra rinse to make sure all the chemicals are out of the fabric.
- Dab dribbles on the baby's clothes with a damp cloth dipped in baking soda.

Take It and Run
Have a pre-packed bag ready to pick up as you go out of the door with the baby. Put in some nappies, a spare set of clothes, baby wipes, a small blanket and plastic bags (those that come on a roll are handy). A two-foot square of plastic or washable vinyl wallpaper can be put down anywhere to do quick changes. If you are given any free samples of baby products save them for your bag and keep the containers and refill them from larger sizes when they are empty. Keep a clean feeding bottle in the bag, with some dry baby milk powder in it (or water if you're breastfeeding). You might also include a pillowcase to pop a blanket-wrapped baby in for extra warmth in the winter and to stop blanket fluff getting on your clothes. And don't forget to refill your bag as soon as you are back from an outing.

A STIMULATING ENVIRONMENT

Gradually, your whole house will become baby- and child-orientated, but the baby's room will probably be the one of most interest to him or her. Remember that new-born babies can focus their eyes only on objects 7 to 12 inches away. By three months a baby can focus well on more distant objects. Get down to your baby's level often, on a bed or the floor, so that you don't always look like a giant.

World within sight and sound

- Use as much colour in the baby's room as you can with paint, curtains and pictures. Buy or make a bright coloured patchwork quilt; use printed sheets on the cot (normal double sheets, folded in half, work well — they can be very colourful and can be used later, on a big bed). Remember that infants see the colours red and yellow best and that faces, especially those with prominent eyes, are 'readable' to them. Cheer yourself up and stimulate your baby by wearing bright, patterned clothes.

- Make a colourful fabric cover for a vinyl-covered cot bumper, both to protect the vinyl, which tears easily, and to make it more attractive.
- Decorate a wall with a montage of baby congratulation cards or frame some cards to hang up separately. Or hang some attractive plastic placemats.
- Put bright transfers on the inside of the crib, cot or pram.
- Put a colourful poster, kite or piece of wallpaper on the ceiling above the changing table.
- Put a small cork board over the changing table for an older child to display bright drawings for the baby.
- Keep a music box in the baby's room to appeal to the sense of sound, or hang a musical mobile over the cot.
- Put your baby's bouncing cradle on the floor, where he or she can see more. And put a mirror tile on the wall nearby — fun for your infant now and for your crawling child later.
- Hang some of the baby's toys and rattles on the cot with snap-on plastic shower curtain hooks. They're bright and strong; they keep toys in view and off the floor.
- Or attach small stuffed animals to the cot bumper with small pieces of Velcro.
- Decorate your baby's highchair with a colourful picture or transfer, covered with two coats of clear varnish to make it permanent.

Mobiles

- Hang a mobile in the baby's room to encourage eye movement and awareness of surroundings, and remember that the baby will see the *underside* of it. Use *firm* cord — elastic is not safe for a baby who can reach it and a mobile on

a thin string can fly away from a baby's reach or even be pulled down.

- Or let your older child construct a mobile for his or her new brother or sister. It could be made of butterflies cut out of polystyrene food containers and coloured with felt tip pens. Use strong cotton or fishing line to thread through them and attach the butterflies to drinking straws suspended from coat hangers.
- Hang silver spoons from shoelaces to make a mobile that sparkles and makes a charming, tinkling sound when it moves.

Social Life with Your Baby
Remember to serve only finger foods that can be eaten with one hand when you have a party with other parents and their new babies - everyone will have a baby on one arm!

SAVING MONEY ON EQUIPMENT

It's not necessary for parents to buy *every* available piece of equipment for babies; there are many workable substitutes, especially during the first few months of an infant's life, when changes take place so quickly.

- Use a padded laundry basket for a comfortable, portable bed.
- Take the baby's bath for sleeping away from home, or pad a deep drawer for the baby to sleep in when you're visiting.
- Use a pram for an infant bed. It can be gently rocked, whereas a cot can't.
- Substitute a small inflatable plastic paddling pool for a playpen for a child who's not yet crawling.
- Consider propping your baby up in a bean-bag chair occasionally instead of in an infant seat. The chair will be a practical addition to the child's room later, anyway.

YOUR BABY'S SIBLINGS

If there is an older child in your family, he or she will no doubt be excited at the prospect of a new baby. You'll want to talk about the baby while it is in your uterus, as the child once was, and to let the child feel the baby's movements. And you'll want to talk about the baby as it will be — sleeping, crying, eating, taking up a lot of Mummy's time. Make sure your older child doesn't expect an instant playmate.

Preparing the older sibling

- Move the older child on a step or two *before* the baby arrives — to a big bed from a cot, to another bedroom, to nursery school or to play school for one or two days a week — so that these changes won't be seen as rejections after the baby arrives.
- Invite another baby for a few visits so your child will see what it's going to be like. You'll get some practice, too, and the visiting baby's parents will owe you a favour later on.
- Before the baby is born you'll probably be allowed to visit the maternity ward where you'll be. If possible take your child with you and this will give you a chance to talk to your

child about who will be looking after him or her while you're in hospital.

- Take your child with you to an ante-natal check-up to hear the baby's heartbeat, if your doctor's agreeable.
- Give the child a new baby doll to play with and look after, if he or she wants one.
- Involve Daddy actively. If he will be looking after the older child at home, get him to tell the child how happy he'll be when they spend that time together.
- *And don't start any of this too early!* The nine months may seem to go slowly for you, but for a child they are an eternity.

While you're away

- Tape record some stories for your child to listen to while you're in hospital.
- Leave a picture of yourself in your child's room.
- Prepare some little presents to be handed out each day while you're away.
- Send home little presents from the hospital.
- Give the child at home a personal snapshot of the new baby.
- Don't walk in carrying the baby when you go home, if possible; be prepared to devote a few minutes to the older child.

- Ask your older child to take care of something special for you while you're in hospital — perhaps a scarf or piece of jewellery.
- Ring your child frequently from hospital, especially if children are not allowed to visit the maternity ward.

Helping siblings deal with jealousy

It's important to understand that for your older child the trauma of a rival is very real. Jealousy may not appear until the baby is older and develops a real personality, but it's a good idea to be prepared for it. You may want to let any temporary regression by the older child run its course with as little notice and comment as possible, while praising any particularly grown-up behaviour. Don't expect the child to love the baby instantly. Make it clear that hurting the baby is not allowed, but also that adoration is not required.

- Express your own occasional annoyance with the baby's demands to your older child, but not so often that he or she gets the idea that the new sibling is a permanent nuisance. Express your joy, too.
- Put a stool next to the baby's changing table so that your older child can watch changing and dressing routines.
- Let the child help as much as possible with 'our baby', holding, singing or talking to the baby and running errands around the house for you. Show your appreciation for the help.
- Put the baby's cot mattress at the lowest position so that an older child won't be able to try to pick him or her up.
- 'Stall' visitors who come to see the baby so that the older child can be the centre of attention for a few minutes. Show pictures of the child as well as of the baby. Then let the child help you show the baby off.
- Give the older child new privileges: a later bedtime, increased pocket money, special things to do with a parent.
- Get out photos of the older child as a baby, especially those that show you giving him or her the same kind of attention you now give the baby.
- Let the baby give the older child a gift when you go home

from the hospital. Keep a few small surprise gifts ready to give to your older child when visitors bring gifts for the baby.

- Teach the older child that if he or she smiles at the baby often, the infant will soon return the smile. And show the child how to touch, love and cuddle the baby.

The Other Kind of 'Sibling'
To help the family dog or cat adjust to the new baby, place a nappy or blanket with the baby at the hospital (make sure the staff know your plan so it won't be washed). The day before the baby is brought home, give the cloth to the pet to play with and sniff - the baby's odour will then be a familiar one. You can 'pet proof' the baby's room by putting a gate across the door; you'll still be able to see into the room but pets will be kept out.

YOUR BABY'S DOCTOR

Some parents question the need for routine check-ups for healthy babies. But in the long run, they often save trouble and worry because problems can be diagnosed early. A continuing medical history of a child is also often valuable if problems develop later in his or her life.

Seeing the doctor

- Keep a note-pad in a convenient place in your home to make notes of questions you want to ask at the check-up. Also note your baby's 'history', including sleeping, crying and eating patterns, bowel habits and such.

- Don't be afraid to ask *anything*. A foolish question is better than a mistake.
- Write down any instructions the doctor or health visitor give you; what seems perfectly clear at the surgery or clinic may become less so by the time you get home.
- Save yourself trouble by putting a disposable nappy on the baby, even if you normally use terry ones. You won't have to take a wet or soiled nappy home. And take masking tape with you so you can reuse the nappy if it's still dry.

Reasons to call the doctor

- The first occurrence of any illness new to the baby — even a cold.
- Diarrhoea, when bowel movements are more watery and more frequent than usual.
- Blood-tinged urine or bowel movements.
- Poor feeding, when the baby stops the usual vigorous sucking during feeds.
- Unusual crying that continues, or a hoarse, husky cry.
- A significant change in the baby's usual colour, breathing, behaviour or activity.
- A rectal temperature of 101 degrees or higher.
- If the baby is usually active and alert and slowly becomes listless and takes no interest in anything; or drowsiness at an unusual time, lasting for a long time.
- Convulsions, 'fits' or spells during which the child stiffens or twitches uncontrollably.
- Discharge from the ears or ear ache, shown by constant turning of the head or pulling at the ear or crying when coughing.
- Forceful vomiting instead of the usual bringing up of food.
- A serious-looking rash — one that covers a large part of the baby's body and is unfamiliar to you.
- Redness of or discharge from the baby's eyes.
- Any injury from which the pain or disability doesn't disappear within 15 minutes.

Chapter Two

Child Care: the Basics

The routines of feeding, clothing and getting your child to sleep move slowly from things you do for them to things you help them do for themselves. While it often seems easier to do it all yourself, you'll want to encourage as much self-help as possible.

FEEDING

If you worry about getting the baby to eat — *don't*. It's not really possible to make a baby eat. You can control the quality and variety that you offer, but the baby should control the quantity that's taken in. Remember that a child's appetite usually decreases dramatically at about one year of age.

Try to make eating fun, and remember to monitor your own facial expression when feeding a child. If you turn your nose up at spinach, your child will instantly decide that he or she doesn't like it.

Feeding the baby

- Warm baby food in an egg poacher, using the cups for different foods.
- Use paper cups for suitable baby foods and save washing up.
- Puree foods in a blender or food mill in bulk and freeze them in ice cube trays (or in mounds on baking sheets),

then transfer to plastic bags. Cubes thaw quickly and are easy to take with you for meals when you're out.

- Feed a young child with a banana straight from the skin, with a spoon, one piece at a time. The rest of the banana will stay fresh and not turn brown.
- Add a little liquid to soft-cooked meats to make them easier to grind in a blender. In the same blender you can puree most of your own foods, unseasoned, for your baby.
- Use a long-handled spoon that fits the baby's mouth. Tender gums like the feel of plastic-coated spoons.

When There's No Highchair

'Trap' a small child for feeding (when a highchair's not available or the child is too small for one) and still provide comfort: cross your left leg over your right knee at the ankle, forming a triangle. (Reverse the position if you are left-handed.) Put the child in the triangle. He or she can't get out and wriggle. A bonus is that you can feed the child while you are eating your own meal.

- Stop the baby sliding down in a highchair by putting a rubber mat or a baby's safety bath mat on the seat, or secure the baby with a harness.
- Or use a commercially-made highchair cushion which helps a very young child sit up.

- Try using a moulded plastic bib with a pocket to catch the spills. Or try a 'coverall' bib to keep the baby's clothes clean. If the bib isn't waterproof on at least one side, use it just for dribbles.
- If vinyl bibs irritate the baby's skin, sew them to the backs of terry ones. They'll be soft under the baby's chin, but still waterproof.
- Tuck a double thickness of facial or toilet tissue under the neckline of the bib to stop dribbles running down the baby's neck.
- Watch out and *duck* if the baby sneezes with a mouthful of food!

Do-it-yourself eaters

Self-feeding is messy, and it often takes a child a long time to eat even a small meal, but you should encourage it anyway. Don't worry if your child prefers fingers to spoons; they're faster, and feeling food is as important to a child as is its colour and flavour. The finer points of etiquette can be learned later. Just make things as easy as possible for the child (and yourself) and let him or her get on with it.

- Put a rubber suction soap holder on the tray to stop the plate or bowl slipping and to leave both the baby's hands free for eating.

- Put the baby's food straight onto the highchair tray first of all to avoid the problem of the thrown plate.
- Try a colourful scarf for a child who doesn't like wearing a rigid feeder. The folds may catch some of the spills.
- Give a child who insists on eating from a big plate a plastic one with a raised rim. Some even have divided sections.
- Give the baby a spoon in each hand and use one yourself. The baby will imitate you. Teaspoons and hors d'oeuvres forks (not too sharp!) are easy for babies to eat from. And for a real beginner, consider using a wooden tongue depresser as a scoop for food.
- Give a plastic picnic knife and fork to a child who wants all the tools for eating that grown-ups have.

Do-it-yourself drinkers

- Slip a bright-coloured sock over the bottle to make it easier for the baby to hold.
- Let a toddler learn to drink from a cup in the bath.
- Or let the child drink from a plastic medicine or eyewash cup. They're easier to hold and won't soak the child if they get spilt. For a change you could try small paper cups.
- Fill toddlers' glasses only about a third full to prevent waste if they're spilt.
- Draw or tape a circle on the highchair tray to show your child where the cup goes, but not too close to the edge.
- Let your child use a bright-coloured straw, or several of them, for drinking sometimes. Cut straws off two inches above the cup so the child won't tip the drink over.

Easy eating

- If your child pesters you while you're preparing a meal, give him or her a small paper bag of things that he or she can pull out to feel and eat.
- Give your child cereal or soup in a cup or mug with a handle to hold. Milk or soup left over can be drunk instead of spooned out.

- Quickly cool food that's too hot for a toddler by dropping an ice cube into it.
- Divide a bun tin or ice cream container into sections with different finger foods such as cheese cubes, strips of cold meat, crackers, raw vegetables or fruit. It's called a 'pot pourri lunch'.
- Occasionally serve a meal on a doll's plate, an aluminium pie plate or a new Frisbee, just for fun.
- Mix yoghurt or apple sauce instead of milk with dry cereal to make a manageable solid food for a child who hasn't yet mastered handling a spoon.
- Serve wholemeal rolls slightly frozen — they're nutritious, and make fewer crumbs.
- Use pureed meat or vegetables a baby won't eat as sandwich spreads; finger foods often go down more easily than those which have to be eaten with a spoon.
- Or mash leftovers, mix them with an egg and cook like pancakes, or bake them on cake trays.
- Fill an ice cream cone with tuna or egg salad, cottage cheese or yoghurt to make them easier to eat. They make a good lunch, too, for an older child who's out playing.
- Let a pre-school child make a 'dangerous dinner'. It's constructed with toothpicks held together with pieces of meat, chunks of cheese and vegetables, dried fruits — anything good. When it's 'built', it's ready to eat.
- Teach even young children to get a cold meal for themselves — a sandwich or a ready prepared salad from the refrigerator — so they can be self-sufficient sometimes.

Teething aids

- *Frozen water-filled teething rings; chilled dummies.*
- *A chilled seedless orange, cut into sections. Or unpeeled chunks of apple or other fruits. (Beware of large chunks that a child with a few teeth might bite off and choke on.)*
- *A cold or frozen carrot or stringless cold celery. (See note of caution above.)*
- *A frozen banana, or a lengthwise-cut piece of one.*

- *A cold or frozen roll.*
- *A dampened flannel or soft cloth frozen and put in a plastic bag.*
- *An ice cube, tied in a flannel with string.*
- *A toothbrush.*
- *A clean rubber ring.*
- *Or a dog biscuit - really! They're not harmful in any way.*

Cleaning up: your child

- Take your child to the sink using the 'rugby hold' (tucked under your arm) and make a game of washing hands and face after meals.
- Keep a step-stool handy for a child old enough to wash his or her own hands and face at the sink.
- Use your hand, dipped in water, to wash the face of a reluctant toddler. Most children don't seem to fight as much as if you use a cloth, and you'll do just as good a job.
- Let your child dip messy hands into a plastic bowl of water while still in the highchair. Then just wipe them dry.
- Squirt a little shaving cream on the child's cheeks and let him or her 'shave' it off with a flannel.

Cleaning-up: equipment

- Put a plastic tablecloth or a playmat on the floor under the highchair, if you have kitchen carpeting, and you'll be able to wipe up spills easily. On a hard-surface floor, spread out a newspaper and pull off one page after each meal, wrapping the crumbs inside. Or get a non-finicky dog.
- Put a lightweight paper towel holder, or one with suction cups, on the back of the highchair to hold towels for quick mop-ups.
- Buy a highchair with a detachable tray, if you're getting a new one, for quick, easy cleaning.
- Rub waxed paper over the runners of a clean highchair to make the tray slide back on more easily. Or apply a little petroleum jelly or salad oil with a cotton wool ball.

- Put a plastic and metal highchair under the shower and let hot water spray over it for a few minutes. Caked-on food wipes off easily.
- Clean the highchair outdoors in the summer with the garden hose. Leave it in the sun for a while to help disinfect it.
- Use a solution of water and washing up liquid to loosen really crusty spills.
- Give your child a plastic ice cream carton and a sponge and let him or her help.

CLOTHING

As soon as possible, begin giving your child choices about clothes. Having a choice of three outfits can make all the difference to having a finicky youngster and, to one who doesn't care, it provides practice in making decisions. Thereby begins the process of establishing a self-image.

When you choose clothes for your child, you'll want to consider comfort, fit and durability. If you can't resist a frill, bow or piece of lace, make sure it's firmly attached (and wash the garment before it's worn, if the decoration is likely to irritate). Remember that knitted garments are easier to care for than woven fabrics and more comfortable to wear. Front fasteners will be easier for your child (and for you, when you have to dress a child who won't stand still). Necklines in slip-over clothing must be large enough to slip over the child's head without a struggle. Pre-school children need plenty of pockets for collecting things.

When you're doing the dressing

- Buy dungarees with fasteners in the crotch for easy nappy changing.
- To distract a baby who's old enough to resist having it's nappy changed do it while he or she is standing up, perhaps watching television.
- Or talk to the child very quickly, so that he or she will have to pay close attention to your face, not your hands.
- Give the child a toothbrush or a toy to play with, or stick some masking tape on his or her fingers — it'll take a minute or two to get off.
- Or put up mirror tiles where a child can see himself or herself and share the boredom of nappy changing with a 'friend'.
- Dress a wriggly toddler on his or her tummy, if you can, to give you better control.
- Fasten dungaree straps together across the back to stop them sliding down a toddler's arm.
- Choose clothes with zippers rather than buttons to make dressing a child who won't keep still easier.
- Run a bar of soap (the little ones from hotels are ideal) or a lead pencil over a sticking zipper.
- Put a small treat, such as a grape or a piece of rusk, into your child's hand so he or she will clench the fist to push through a sleeve.
- Ask your child to clench his or her fist when you're putting on mittens. When the mitten's on, ask the child to stick out the thumb first, then open the fist.
- Attach mittens to a long string that goes through both coat sleeves.
- Use knee-high socks as mittens — they can't be pulled off.
- Don't be surprised if the toddler you've just dressed has taken off all his or her clothes within minutes. That's a skill to be mastered, too. (One-piece garments will help discourage undressing, if you really haven't time for it.)

Night-time nappying

- Double nappy the baby, if you use terry nappies, or put a sanitary towel (or part of one) inside a nappy.
- Use half of a cheap disposable nappy, with the tabs cut off and plastic perforated, as a liner to make a better night-time disposable nappy.
- Slip one disposable nappy into another that you've split at the top, with both plastic pieces on the outside.
- Use rubber or plastic pants over nappies, if your child doesn't have nappy rash.

Putting shoes on

- Put shoes on a fidgety toddler while the child is in the highchair. Or lightly tickle the bottom of the child's foot — toes will uncurl and shoes will go on smoothly.
- Wet shoelaces before tying them and as they shrink they'll tighten up and stay tied.
- Prevent the tongues of shoes from sliding out of place by cutting two small parallel slits in each tongue, a half-inch from the outside edge. Pull the laces through the slots and tie as normal.
- Spray the insides of boots with a dusting product containing wax and wipe until dry. The boots will slip on easily.

Daily use of footwear

- Stick T-shaped pieces of adhesive tape on the bottoms of a baby's new hard-soled shoes to give more grip and help a young walker gain confidence. Or simply rough up the surface of the shoe sole with sandpaper.
- Repair rubber boots with materials from an inexpensive inner-tube repair kit, available from a car accessories shop.
- Use your hair dryer to dry winter boots quickly.

Save Time... Save Pyjamas
If you can bring yourself to break old habits, dress your children in clean clothes at bedtime. Today's fabrics don't crease and the children are ready to go out in the morning.

Dressing themselves: fastenings

You'll want to encourage every effort your child makes to dress him or herself, even though it'll take a great deal more time at first and cause some frustration for both you and the child. If you can't resist helping, busy yourself elsewhere, close enough to be of assistance if needed, but giving the child a chance to do it alone.

- Make button-handling easier by sewing large buttons on your child's clothes and easier still by sewing them on with elastic thread.
- Teach your child to button from the bottom up; the chances of getting it right are better.
- Tie big wooden beads, buttons or small toys to the strings of hoods to stop the strings being pulled out.
- Attach curtain rings to zippers on boots and jackets to make them more manageable. On boots, the rings can be hooked together when they're put away.
- Teach your child to pull a zipper away from clothes and skin to stop it from catching.

Dressing themselves: other aids

- Buy trousers and skirts with elasticized waistbands to make them easy to pull on and off, but make sure the elastic isn't so tight that it leaves marks on the skin or rides up.
- Mark the belt hole a child should use with a piece of masking or adhesive tape.
- Try to get clothing with monograms, appliques or other special trim on the front to help a child tell the front from the back. On homemade clothes, mark an X in the back with coloured thread.
- Teach your child to look for the label in the back of underpants. If there's no label, indicate the front by sewing on a 'belly button' or drawing one with a marking pen.
- Sew loops of elastic thread inside the cuffs of sweaters and get your child to loop them over his or her thumbs to hold the sleeves down while putting on a coat or jacket.
- Help your child to put on a jacket or coat: spread the garment on the floor, openings up, and get the child to

stand at the neck end, bend over, slip arms into sleeves and flip it over his or her head. Or get the child to lie on his or her back on the garment, put arms in armholes and stand up.

XYZ!
You have a boy who's often caught with his zipper down? Say 'XYZ' to him - 'Examine your zipper.' Add 'PDQ' - 'Pretty damn quick!'

Helping with shoes

There is no need for toddlers to wear shoes — going barefoot gives little feet good exercise. For a child a little older, new shoes are often a great source of pleasure. They can also be a source of frustration. To help your child distinguish between the right and left shoes, mark the inside edges of both shoes with a piece of tape or a felt tip pen; when the marks match, the shoes are on the right feet. Or explain that if the toes point 'in', the shoes 'like each other' and are happy; turning away from each other makes them sad.

- Point the ends of shoelaces with clear nail polish or wrap masking tape round them when the plastic tips wear off.
- Tie knots at the ends of laces after lacing the shoes. The child can take the shoes off easily but won't pull the laces out.
- Avoid lacing and tying problems by substituting quarter-inch elastic for laces. Sew the ends together at the top. The elastic stretches so that the shoe can be slipped on and off without untying.
- Keep shoelaces even at the ends by folding them in half and tying a knot in the middle.
- Help a pre-school child learn to tie shoes by letting him or her practice with one red and one black liquorice string, which will let him or her see which one is going over or under which. Success means, of course, that the child is allowed to eat the liquorice.

Keeping clothes organized

- Hang coordinated sets of clothes in the wardrobe or put complete outfits together in drawers so that your child can pick out matching outfits.

- Organize socks for more than one child by giving each a special pattern or colour, or by buying a different make for each.
- Buy all the same make and colour socks for an only child to save having to match them up.
- Pin pairs of small socks together with nappy pins for washing and storage, and 'pin' them to the clothes-line.
- Use sew-on name tags for marking instead of iron-on ones, which tend to come off after three or four washings.
- Or mark with an indelible pen or an inexpensive rubber stamp that you can have made up at a stationery store.
- Write names on dark-coloured boots and plimsolls with a cotton bud dipped in bleach or with red gloss paint, which lasts longer than nail polish. If you prefer to mark inside the boots, use a marking pen.

Hand-me-downs

- Mark borrowed babies' or children's clothes that are to be returned so that you'll remember who lent them to you. And label things *you* lend and want returned.
- Sort hand-me-downs according to season and size and label the boxes you keep them in. Use disposable nappy boxes which state weight or size to store baby clothes of that size and other small items. Really precious baby things — those you want to keep forever — will keep better in plastic bags fastened with wire closures.
- Make boys' hand-me-downs feminine for girls by embroidering initials on pockets and designs around collars or cuffs and/or sewing on appliqués.
- Mark clothes with a single X or dot for the oldest child, two for the next, and so on. When clothes are handed down, it's easy to add another mark.
- Mark sizes on the inside of waistbands of trousers if labels have come off or become unreadable.
- Use only the family surname for marking outer clothes that you're sure will be handed down from one child to another.
- Avoid resentment over hand-me-downs by calling them

'school dresses' or 'first size trousers' instead of 'Susie's' or 'Jimmy's'.

- Organize a hand-me-down evening at your church or at someone's house. Pass around a box and people can put in what they no longer need and take out what they do.

Wise shopping for clothing

Some of the best-dressed children have the least amounts of money spent on their clothes. Sales, charity shops, discount stores and jumble sales account for some savings. Hand-me-downs from relatives and friends also help. Clever shoppers try to keep a little spare cash for an unexpected opportunity. Carrying a small notebook with measurements and sizes of all family members helps, too, and remember that for small children height and weight measurements are often more important than sizes. Remember to update your notebook.

- Don't buy plastic pants with poppers; they pull off too easily.
- Buy 'neutral' jeans, shirts and outer clothing so that they can be passed on to children of different sexes.
- Get 'unisex' clothing in boys' departments; it's usually made of stronger material and often costs less than that in girls' departments.
- Look for the best quality in everyday wear such as underwear and items which will be passed on to several children.

- Check for the fit of socks if you aren't sure of the size. Ask the child to clench its fist and wrap the sock around the fist over the knuckles. If the heel and toe meet, the sock will fit.
- Buy shoes with laces for small children. Little slip-ons look nice and are easy to put on, but they don't *stay* on.
- If you always keep to the same colour and make of pyjamas, you can save good parts of worn-out ones for patches.
- Or consider using bright T-shirts with iron-on transfers or embroidery for nightshirts.
- Buy smock-type dresses for girls; when they're too short they can be used as tops to be worn over trousers!

- Remember, when you buy snowsuits, that while one-piece garments are easier to put on, two-piece suits can be worn for longer.

Home-sewn

'Get a good sewing machine and learn to use it, and learn to knit and crochet,' is the advice of many parents who want their children to be dressed well and economically. Work ahead of the seasons, they advise; think about hats and mittens and jackets in the summer, shorts and sun dresses after Christmas. Don't turn up the hems until it's time for the garments to be worn.

When you choose patterns and fabrics, try to imagine the finished product on your child. A style that suits the child's build and personality will look good and will contribute to his or her self-confidence. As the child grows, make notes on favourite patterns about larger waists and longer waists and sleeves. Remember that the fewer the seams and built-in detail, the easier the garment will be to make and the better it will look and wear. You can allow for growth by choosing styles with raglan or dolman sleeves and, in one-piece garments, with undefined waistlines. If you make double-breasted coats and jackets, you can realign buttons as the child grows.

- *Always* wash all fabric before cutting to allow for shrinkage and in case the colours run. Use the water temperature and drying method you'll use for the finished garment.

- Sew on shank buttons and metal dungaree buttons with dental floss to stop them being torn off.

- Put extra buttons on dungaree straps at various lengths. As the child grows, the old ones can simply be snipped off. And sew double rows of poppers or buttons on two-piece sleepwear for the same reason.

- Apply clear nail polish over the tops of small buttons to help stop them coming off and perhaps ending up in a small child's mouth.

- Avoid sewing on buttons when you know you'll have to move them as the child grows. Sew thread through button eyes as if you're sewing the button onto material. Attach the buttons to the garment with safety pins run through the thread on the back . . . and re-pin as necessary.

- Sew an extra button or two to a piece of fabric from a garment and keep it in your button box so you'll know where to find it when you need it.
- Sew an extra button under the hem of a front-buttoning garment so that you'll have a matching one when the garment is lengthened.

- Use sellotape or masking tape when you're measuring and marking hems; it won't pinch or prick your child like pins.
- Save hand sewing by using iron-on bonding materials for hems in lightweight fabrics.
- Put a long zipper from top to crotch in dungarees for a boy who's toilet trained. A standard fly is usually hard to manipulate.
- Sew a cardigan inside a coat as an extra liner.
- Make matching T-shirts (for siblings or for look-alike fun with friends or cousins) from one length of 150 cm-wide fabric.
- Use long dressmakers' pins with coloured plastic heads for sewing. They're easy to find and wonderful to sew with. Some mothers even count pins when sewing with small children around.
- Use empty vitamin bottles or other small containers with childproof caps to store pins and other little sewing notions. Contents are easily visible, yet safe from children.

Uses for wonderful Velcro

- In small circles, in place of buttons, down the fronts of shirts and blouses and for waistband closures.
- Instead of buttons, to attach dungaree straps to dungaree bibs.
- Attached to mittens, to stick them together when they're put away.
- On dungaree straps in the back, to stop them slipping down a child's arms.
- On flannels, to make easy-to-change nappies for your child's doll.

- To make a personalized T-shirt, attach tiny stuffed animals or other little toys that your child can take on and off.

Making clothes last longer

- Fold two nappies together to fit an older baby, then stitch along each end to make them 'ready folded'.
- Buy two-piece pyjamas for longer wear.
- Open the bottom seam on an outgrown one-piece baby's sleeping bag and use it for a beach cover-up.
- Turn bobbly old tights inside out. They don't look much different, except that they're smooth again.
- Try tie-dying T-shirts that are badly stained.
- Reinforce the knees on new jeans (on the inside) with the fabric you cut off when you turn them up or with iron-on patches.
- Cut dungarees that are too short apart at the waist and insert a wide band of matching or contrasting fabric.
- Lengthen girls' trousers by sewing on strips of wide ribbon or decorative braid. Add a similar trim or frills to the legs of pyjama trousers or cut off the sleeves and legs to make summer pyjamas.
- Lengthen straps by sewing on extra fabric.
- Add another tier to tiered skirts or blouses, using matching or contrasting fabric.
- Cut off floor-length dresses to make short ones for another year's wear.
- Cut sleeves that are too-short out of an expensive quilted or padded jacket and let your child wear it over a thick sweater.
- To get more wear out of jackets and anoraks sew knitted cuffs (from the haberdashery department of a departmental store) to the ends of the sleeves.

Patching and covering up

- Patch the knees and feet of sleeping suits with pieces of an old towel.

- Cover old hemline marks on skirts or trousers with zigzag stitching or sew-on rickrack or ribbon.
- Run a dark blue crayon or indelible pencil over the white line on turned down jeans.
- Slip a rolled-up magazine into trouser legs to avoid going through both thicknesses of material when pinning on patches.
- Or hold patches in place for stitching by gluing them on first. After sewing, wash the glue out.
- Cover a hole, mend or stain that shows by sewing on an appliqué.

Knit knacks

- Crochet mittens onto the sleeves of a sweater and they'll never get lost or separated.
- Wind left-over yarn from a knitted garment into a hank, tie it loosely and wash it with the garment. It will stay the same colour as the garment and will be ready for mending or lengthening.
- Unravel an outgrown jumper; wind the yarn loosely in hanks and tie in several places; wash. Rolled into balls, it's ready to reuse for a smaller child's garment.
- Use a pattern one size larger than your child needs when you knit or crochet a garment. If it takes a long time to finish, there's a better chance it will still fit.
- Use knitting and crochet patterns that call for cotton or double knitting wool instead of fingering yarn so your work will go faster.

Preventive maintenance

- Spray knees, cuffs and collars of garments with fabric protector (and the fronts of 'best clothes' for a dribbler or messy eater). Spills and such will form into beads and dirt can be wiped off with a damp cloth.
- Sew squares of quilted material on the knees of trousers for crawling babies; they protect both trousers and knees.
- Put iron-on patches on the cotton soles of sleeping suits to stop them wearing out.

Getting clothes clean

Today almost everything but the child goes into the washing machine. Bleach of one kind or another does wonders with really dirty clothes. Some parents change brands of washing powder occasionally, feeling that the new brand washes out the residue of the old, and clothes will be cleaner. If you take your washing to a laundrette, carry your washing powder in old baby food jars to lighten the load you have to take.

And remember — there's no law that says children's play clothes must be spotless!

- Get grimy socks white by soaking them in a solution of washing soda and water before washing. Or boil them in water with a sliced lemon.
- Dip a cotton bud in bleach and dab at stains on white bibs or clothes that have embroidery, appliqué or other unbleachable features.
- Sponge grass stains with alcohol (diluted with two parts water if the fabric is acetate or non-colourfast) if normal washing doesn't get them out. Or work washing up liquid or shampoo into the stain, rinse and wash as usual.
- Soak egg-stained clothing in cold water for an hour before washing. Hot water will set the stain.
- Soak bloodstains in cold water for at least 30 minutes. If the stain doesn't come out, soak in a biological detergent or

pour a few drops of ammonia on the spot. Or try using hydrogen peroxide before soaking in water.

- Soak vomit-stained clothes in cold water and sponge stains with a solution of a quart of ammonia and a half-teaspoon of washing up liquid.
- Remove food colouring stains from clothes by rubbing them with toothpaste. Leave to dry, rinse in cold water and wash as usual.
- Use a cup of vinegar in a gallon of water, or add a tablespoon of dishwasher powder to a load of washing to give a bleach that's safe for nylon, rayon and all fine washables.
- Soak tough stains, such as chocolate or fruit juice, in a solution of one teaspoonful of borax to a pint of water for about ten minutes. Wash as usual afterwards.
- Use carpet shampoo with a brush (and lots of suds) for winter coats that need dry cleaning. It works on both wool and corduroy.
- Remove chewing gum from clothing by softening it with egg white. Scrape it off and wash the garment as usual.

Caring for shoes

- Clean white baby shoes by rubbing them with a raw potato, liquid non-abrasive cleaner or alcohol before polishing. Or apply toothpaste with an old toothbrush, scrub gently and wipe off. Leave to dry before polishing.
- Spray newly polished white baby shoes with hair spray to prevent polish from coming off.
- Use pre-moistened baby wipes to remove black marks from white shoes.
- Polish children's shoes with an old nylon stocking for a good shine. Or let polish dry thoroughly and buff with waxed paper.
- Clean fabric trainers with a soap-filled scouring pad. Use bleach or lemon juice in the rinsing water if the shoes are white.
- Spray new fabric trainers with starch or fabric protector to stop dirt getting embedded in them.

SLEEPING

Getting children to sleep comfortably and without being frightened through the night is a problem most parents seem to have at various times. Just wait, though — teenagers usually sleep very well, and often late in the morning, when you'd like them to be up and about.

Determining bedtime

- Keep bedtime at the same time every night to help establish regular sleeping habits.
- Relieve yourself of the onus of setting bedtime by letting the hands of the clock do the job.
- Set a timer to mark bedtime and let it go off early enough to give a little warning. If the child hurries and is ready early, as a reward you could let him or her read until the set time.
- Have a 'goodnight parade' if you have two or more children. The whole family marches through the house, stopping in the kitchen for a drink of water, in the bathroom for toothbrushing and toileting. The youngest is put to bed first.
- Or get your child to put all its teddies to bed, one by one — and when they're all asleep, he or she will be the *last one* to go to bed.

Helping children get to sleep

- Add a little cereal to the baby's bottle for the last feed.

- Give your older child a protein snack, if needed, before bedtime.
- Spend some quiet time before bedtime — rough-and-tumble play excites a child.
- Take a good long walk with your child before bedtime and follow it with a nice warm bath and some soothing music.
- Continue the sleeping routine you probably started when your child was an infant.
- Put a few favourite dolls or stuffed animals in bed with your child and tell him or her the toys are ready to settle down. The child may cooperate by settling down himself or herself.
- Let even a little child 'read' himself or herself to sleep — lying down — with a pleasant, non-scary book.
- Put soft stereo headphones on your child and let relaxing music induce sleep.
- Try using a tape recording on nights you can't read to your child at bedtime. It can be one you buy, with favourite songs and nursery rhymes, or one you tape yourself, with bedtime stories and lullabies.
- Give your child a relaxing mini-massage.
- If your child likes his or her back rubbed, make it more interesting by 'planting a garden', using different strokes for digging, raking, preparing the rows and planting the fruit and vegetable seeds the child has chosen.
- Teach your child to relax every muscle, starting with the toes and moving up to the head. Eyes should be kept closed.
- Put a dab of cologne on the back of your child's hand and tell him or her to sniff until the scent is gone. Deep breathing and concentration usually bring on sleep quickly.
- Have a nice cuddle with your child before sleeping time, once he or she is in a big bed. It gives a parent a nice little rest and it's an enjoyable tradition to start.
- Let your child pick from a 'dream jar' (perhaps an empty tin you've decorated) a slip of paper on which you've written

an idea for a pleasant dream. The child can go to sleep with the paper under the pillow.

Night wakers

Some parents leave a child who wakes up to cry after making sure there's nothing really wrong, and they say the crying shortens in duration over a few nights and soon stops altogether. If you can't bear to do that, keep in mind that often simply picking up and cuddling a child for a few minutes will do the trick and that night waking doesn't last forever. Ignore the advice of well-meaning friends and relatives whose children 'always slept all night'.

- Give your child a bottle, if you wish, but if he or she has teeth, make it plain water only. Milk or any sweetened drink may lead to severe tooth decay.
- Keep several dummies in the cot, but *never* tie one on a string around a baby's neck. It might get tangled and cause strangulation.
- Take the child back to bed with you. One 'family bed' variation is a king-sized bed with a cot with one side removed pushed up against it. Another is a guard rail on one side of the bed; the parents needn't be separated with a child between them, and there's no worry about the child falling out of bed. For some, family sleeping equals comfort. Those who like the idea (not everyone does) say it fulfils a basic human need for warmth, closeness and security.
- Use an incentive chart for a child if you don't want him or her in your bed. Draw stars on a calendar with marking pens (let the child choose the colour) for each night he or

she doesn't come into your bed. Ten stars could earn a small present.

- Put a small mattress (or a big pillow) and a blanket on the floor near your bed for the night-time waker who wants to go back to sleep near you.
- Use a nightlight in the room if the child wants one, or let the child have a torch flashlight. Or try a lighted fish tank, which offers not only light, but movement as well.
- See your doctor to find out if there's any physical reason for unusually frequent waking. The child may have a middle ear infection. The flat position of sleeping increases the pressure behind the eardrum and causes pain.

Sleepwalkers

- Guide a sleepwalker back to bed, awake or asleep (myths about it being bad to wake a sleepwalker are just that — myths), talking quietly and reassuringly. Stop at the toilet before going back to the child's bedroom, then stay with the child until you are sure he or she is sleeping well again.
- Take precautions: block stairs with gates and put secure locks on doors that lead outside.
- Or put a gate across the child's doorway, or even a chain lock on the outside of the door. Either will allow you to look inside, yet still stop the child getting out.
- If sleepwalking is frequent, see your doctor. There may be a physical reason for it.

Delaying the 'early riser'

- Put a few cloth books or soft toys in a small child's cot for the child to play with in the morning. Make sure you do this, though, after the child is asleep.
- Attach an unbreakable mirror to the inside of the cot so a baby or toddler can amuse himself or herself for a few extra minutes in the morning.
- Leave a 'surprise bag' by the bed of an older child or fasten a bicycle basket or plastic pail to the side of the cot — also after the child is asleep. Put in a selection of small items for quiet play — books, games or things to create with, such as

scraps of material, crayons and paper.

- If your child wakes up hungry add something to eat as long as he or she can handle it and won't make a mess. A good snack that takes a great deal of time is raisins wound up every few inches into a strip of waxed paper and formed into a 'snake'. (Some parents don't leave food out though, in case it attracts flies and other insects.)
- Set an alarm clock or clock radio for a child who always wakes up early. Only when it goes off may he or she get up. Or set two clocks for a pre-schoolchild — one running, the other unwound with the hands pointing to getting-up time. When the two clocks show the same time, the child may get up.

Naps

- Try 'white noise' in a little one's room if older children's playing stops him or her sleeping. Put a small fan on a high cupboard, directing the flow of air away from the child, and let it hum away.
- Make a sleeping nest for a toddler in a large cardboard box decorated with bright drawings or transfers inside and padded comfortably.
- Let your child have a nap in a sleeping bag on your bed, the living room couch or the floor of his or her own room, just for a change.
- Call nap-time by another name such as 'rest time' or 'quiet time' for a child who doesn't want to sleep. Sometimes the child will actually fall asleep, but even if he or she doesn't the time alone will be relaxing.
- Set an alarm clock or timer for a child who's resting, or put on a few long-playing records, to mark the end of rest time.

Going Visiting
The friend you're visiting doesn't have a cot - and your baby needs a sleep. Put the baby in the bath with a cushion or a few towels. Make sure you remove soap and other bathing equipment and do this only with a baby who can't sit up alone or reach the taps. And only if your friend does not have a child old enough to turn on the taps but too young to understand the dangers.

Chapter Three

Hygiene and Health

Parents of young children usually spend a good deal of time in the bathroom... but not by themselves! Trying to keep active children clean, introducing them to the art of cleaning themselves and getting them to use the toilet are time-consuming operations. Here are some ideas to make that time pay off.

SOAP AND WATER

When there are two or more little bodies to be bathed (or even just one), many parents find the assembly line method fast and easy. One parent washes and shampoos, the other dries and assists with pyjamas.

Bathing and shampooing

- Use a clean washing-up liquid bottle as a baby shampoo dispenser. The pull-up top lets you squirt just the right amount and reclose it with one hand.
- Take your child into the shower with you to help him or her get used to water on the head and face.
- If you use a big bath for a baby who can't sit up on its own, put an infant seat into the bath and strap the baby into that.
- Let a toddler play in a small, open mesh plastic laundry basket in the big bath as a transition from the baby bath. The

basket can serve as a place to store the bath toys when the bath is finished.

- Or try using a plastic inflatable pool in the shower also as a transition.

Play in the bath

- Keep bath toys in a nylon net bag and hang it from the taps or shower head to drip dry.
- Make inexpensive, super bath toys by cutting coloured sponges into interesting shapes.
- Let bath time be 'science time' — provide a variety of things that sink and float; plastic glasses tall and thin, short and fat; large and small cups for measuring and pouring.
- If your toddler doesn't like getting out of the bath, pull the plug out. When there's no more water left to play with, he or she will probably get out willingly. Or set a timer to go off when playtime is over.

- Or make two simple rules: 'When you stand up you have to get out' or 'You have to get out when your skin is wrinkled and you look like a raisin.'
- Use the time while your toddler is playing in the bath to clean the rest of the bathroom.

Warning!
Never leave a small child unattended in a bath - even if an older child is present.

Fear of the bath water

- Bath with your child to provide extra security... and besides, it's fun.
- Run the bath water before bringing a frightened child into the bathroom, as long as you don't have another child who might climb in while your back is turned.
- Ask your child to help you put in a non-slip mat, lots of toys and bubble bath, to give him or her something else to think about. Some parents prefer to use a little washing up liquid to make bubbles as bubble bath has been known to contribute to vaginal infection in little girls.
- Use only a few inches of water in the bath, increasing the amount as your child begins to get used to it.
- Empty the bath after the child is out. Some are afraid that they, too, may go 'down the drain'.

Scared of shampooing

Most first-time parents are surprised when this fear develops, yet it's common. Wash the child's hair as seldom as possible during this period — once or twice a week is probably often enough, unless there are special problems. Instead, brush hair frequently, give dry shampoos with a hairbrush covered with an old nylon stocking and occasionally 'wash' hair with a damp flannel. When you want to shampoo, use a baby shampoo and do the job quickly and matter-of-factly, praising your child for being brave. As difficult as this period is for you both, remember that it will pass.

- Wash your child's hair first and then let him or her play so bathtime will end on a happy note.

- Put a little lather on the child's hand and let him or her shampoo a doll while you shampoo the child.
- Make soap sculptures in the hair with shampoo and keep a small mirror handy so that the child can admire them and see what you are doing.
- Try using a no-longer-used infant seat; the tilt allows the child's head to be tipped back comfortably for shampooing.
- Tell your child the story of the speck of dirt that gets tired, settles on the child's head and is joined by lots more specks, only to get washed out by Mum or Dad. The story should last as long as the hair washing does.
- Or sing loud songs together while you are washing the child's hair.
- Wrap the child in a big beach towel and lay him or her on the kitchen sink drainer, face up, with head over the sink. Use a spray, if you have one. The towel holds the child steady, it is easier for you to control the soap and water, and your closeness gives security.
- Put only a small amount of water in the bath so the child can lie down flat for shampooing.
- Fill a big plastic jug with water and let it sink to the bottom of the bath — the child can use it for a headrest.
- Lean the child back under the mixer tap for a quick, easy rinse. Or make things fun by using his or her own little watering can for the rinse.
- Use a sponge instead of a cup to control water when you rinse. (And try a sponge for applying shampoo — soap won't be so likely to run into eyes.)
- Give your child a small folded towel or flannel to hold over his or her face. Or use a shampoo shield or swimming goggles.

To Remove Chewing Gum from Hair
Use peanut butter. Work it into the hair, comb out the chewing gum and peanut butter. Shampoo. Cold cream also works, as do olive oil and witch hazel. (And try baby oil to remove chewing gum from skin, or press a second piece of chewing gum over the first and lift both off together.)

CLEAN AND TIDY

With babies and toddlers, the 'finer points' of grooming are your responsibility and you don't want to encourage self-help with such tools as scissors and cotton buds. As children grow, they often begin to take pleasure in looking and smelling nice. If they start out with good habits, they're more likely to stick to them.

Encouraging good habits

- Keep a sturdy stepstool next to the sink to encourage self-help.
- Hand a small medicine cabinet on the bathroom wall at child's eye level to hold grooming necessities. If the small cabinet is mirrored, so much the better.
- Or buy mirror tiles you can stick on the wall at child height so your child won't have to climb. If possible, position the tiles where you can add additional ones above them as the child grows.
- Give your child a personal hygiene kit, an inexpensive plastic carrying case with his or her name on it. Equip it with a small tube of toothpaste, a toothbrush, a small bar of soap and other necessities.
- A liquid soap dispenser is probably *not* a good idea until

children are about five and will not use it as a plaything.

Using hand towels

The best way to get really dirty hands clean is for a child to wash something in the sink — a toy, a doll, some plastic cups. Remember that you'd really prefer a wet, dirty towel to a neatly hung, unused one.

- Consider giving each member of the family different coloured towels.
- Or buy flannels and hand towels printed with pictures of favourite characters for the children.
- Place press-on hooks at your child's level so that towels can be hung up more easily.
- Attach a hand towel to a towel rail with a shower curtain hook or blanket pin. It will hang securely for drying hands.
- Give a bath mitt to a child who hates washing. Make it out of an old sock tied up with soap inside, or sew two flannels together and put soap inside.

Cutting nails

- Cut an infant's nails at nursing time, with his or her head propped on a pillow so that you have both hands free.
- Cut nails while the infant or child is asleep.
- Use round-ended scissors, for safety's sake. Or try nail clippers; some say they're easier to use than scissors. (Try keeping one on your key ring for quick clips when the baby sleeps while you're out.)
- Put talcum powder in your palm and scrape your child's nails over it. Enough will stick under the nails to show you how far to cut without hurting.
- Put a fidgety toddler in the highchair and give him or her something to eat. Or cut nails after a meal, when the child is sleepy and content.
- Let your child watch television, as a distraction, while you cut his or her nails.
- Or try filing a child's nails.

- When nail-cutting is finished, clean under little nails with a flat wooden toothpick.

Cutting hair

Keep in mind that time is of the essence when cutting hair. Use sharp scissors. What can't be done in five minutes probably won't get done. Try to insist that haircutting is a job for adults *only*. If your pre-schoolchild abides by this rule, you'll be lucky!

- Cut a baby's hair while he or she is asleep. You may not end up with a super style, but the bulk of it will be off without any fuss.
- Call a haircut a 'trim'. Cuts hurt!
- Sit a child in a highchair or on a high stool for the job — outdoors in the summer. Spread newspaper to catch falling hair even outdoors, because hair doesn't disintegrate as garden clippings do.
- Wrap a child in a large beach towel or small sheet when cutting hair to stop it falling down the child's neck and making it itchy.
- Put transparent sticky tape across a fringe and cut evenly above it.
- Try placing a piece of cardboard or paper between the child's hair and forehead when cutting hair to keep hair clippings and the cold scissors away from the face.
- Or let the child wear a Halloween mask, which will keep hair out of eyes. Make sure you have a mirror handy so the child can admire the effect.
- Try cutting hair with electric hair clippers (they tickle). If Mum cuts Dad's hair with them too, it helps to see that *he* isn't scared.
- When home haircutting becomes a struggle (between parent and child or parent and parent) it's time to change tactics and take your child to a barber. Consider going to one who specializes in cutting childen's hair, at least for the first couple of times, to get your child used to the idea.
- Prepare a child for a first professional haircut by letting him or her watch you or another child having a haircut.

DENTAL CARE

Diet is the first line of defence for good dental care; snacks between meals and highly sugared foods contribute to decay. Frequent brushings remove the plaque that leads to decay. Brushing after snacks, even healthy ones like raisins or fruit juice, is particularly important. Toddlers and pre-school children, however enthusiastic, need help with toothbrushing; the manual dexterity necessary to clean every surface of every tooth doesn't develop until the age of six or seven. To show your child where plaque collects on teeth and where decay can start, use a disclosing solution that you can buy at the chemist.

Your child's routine dental check-ups should begin, dentists recommend, when two or three teeth have come through. Most parents take their children to their usual family dentist. It is as important for a dentist to look at the shape of a child's mouth — to check the child's bite — as to check for cavities.

Toothbrushing routines

- Consider cleaning your infant's first tooth or two with a small gauze pad, with or without toothpaste. Rub the pad over the teeth and gums very gently to remove plaque and food debris. You'll probably find it easier to do this with the child's head on your lap.
- Let your child use an electric toothbrush if you have one and he or she likes the vibration. The cordless kinds are the easiest to handle. At least let him or her use the little brush — it's small enough to fit a tiny mouth.
- Offer a selection of toothbrushes in all colours, and one or more toothpastes that the child likes. The small samples or travel sizes are favourites. If you find that mint flavoured toothpastes are too strong for your child's sensitive taste buds, try using specially prepared baby toothpaste.
- Try using an egg timer and make a rule that brushing must continue until the sand is through. Or use a kitchen timer set for a specific length of time, or, for a change, a musical box or a record.
- Let the child clean his or her teeth in the bath sometimes, where he or she can spit, dribble and gargle to his or her heart's content.

- Let your children clean their teeth with you, both for the company and so you can set an example. Some children are even allowed to brush their parents' teeth so they can perfect their techniques.
- Have a small mirror at the child's eye level so he or she can watch.
- Get across the idea that the tooth fairy pays a lot more for a perfect tooth than for a decayed one at an *early* age. In some families the fairy leaves a note with the 'payment' praising the child for good dental habits.

TOILET TRAINING

While you may wish to choose the time to toilet train your child (obviously spring and summer are the most convenient seasons), remember that no child will be trained until he or she is ready — perhaps at 24 to 27 months or even older. Some of the signs of readiness are dry nappies for a couple of hours at a time; ability to understand simple commands and explanations and to mimic adults at other bathroom routines, such as brushing teeth or washing hands; an inclination towards tidiness, such as lining up shoes or toys neatly; and dislike of being wet or soiled.

Remember that if you try to hurry things you'll only be training yourself. Put the whole thing off for a few weeks or months if it doesn't seem to be working. Relax, and don't pay too much attention to friends' and relatives' advice. By the time your child goes to school, you'll wonder why toilet training seemed such a big thing.

Basic training

Help your child to understand that once basic training is underway, toilet habits are his or her own responsibility, including cleaning up after accidents. Make it clear that this is not a punishment — just a matter of looking after oneself.

- Put the potty in the bathroom or toilet some months before you think your child will be ready to use it. Explain that when he or she is old enough, it will be there to use.
- Try letting your child go without bottom clothing altogether, when training starts, to make things easier for you both. (You'll have to be a little brave to do this, or at least be a really good observer!)
- Make potty cleaning easier for yourself right from the beginning by putting an inch or so of water in the bottom.
- Let your child learn by watching you or an older child. (If the potty is put near the toilet, you can go together.) Imitation seems to be especially attractive to boys.
- Buy oversized, inexpensive pants to make pulling up and down easy. They sometimes shrink as much as two or three sizes after washing. The extra absorbency of expensive pants won't prevent them from becoming soaked if you're not using rubber pants over them. You might, however, prefer the specially designed trainer pants which are available from most baby stores. Made from terry-towelling with a waterproof backing, any soiling is contained within the pants.
- Take a potty in the back of the car, so you can stop along the road instead of having to worry about finding a petrol station in a hurry. A little boy can do nicely with an empty plastic bottle.
- Consider using an incentive chart, with stars or other stickers to mark days or parts of days without accidents, as

you may do for other accomplishments. Some parents keep a supply of small toys in a big glass bowl, where they can be easily seen, to use as daily rewards for successful toileting.

- Turn on the taps and let the water run for a few minutes; sometimes the sound of running water will bring 'inspiration'.

Using the big toilet

Some children are afraid of the big toilet. Explaining the body waste process and showing the child the sewer pipes and other plumbing may help overcome fears.

- Let a child who has a potty use the big toilet occasionally so he or she can use one comfortably when not at home.
- Teach a little girl to sit backwards on the big toilet (some boys even like this position) or to perch on it sideways. And supply a step stool to help her climb up and down.
- Give a little boy a box to stand on in front of the toilet. Be specific in teaching him to aim before starting to urinate, perhaps by floating a piece of tissue in the toilet as a target.
- If a box isn't available, let a boy kneel backwards on the seat, facing the back of the toilet.

Bedwetting

Night-time wetting, which can continue into the pre-school years (and beyond, more often for boys than for girls), is frustrating for child and parent alike. It's wise to check with your doctor to make sure there are no underlying physical causes for it. A recent report indicates that bedwetting for some children may be related to an allergic response to cows' milk. For others, it's simply that they're at an age of very sound sleep, during which a child doesn't 'read' the body's signals. In this case, it's usually just a matter of waiting. It's really the child's problem, parents should remember — but there are a few ways to make things easier.

- Protect the child's mattress and, if necessary, the pillow too, with a zippered plastic cover. Or slip the old waterproof sheet from the cot or an old plastic tablecloth between the bottom sheet and the mattress.
- Consider making up the child's bed with two sets of

bedding, including two rubber sheets, so you need only remove one set for a dry bed in the middle of the night.

- Try getting the child up in the night to go to the toilet before you go to bed. This won't *cure* bedwetting, but it may save a wet bed.
- Restrict fluids during the late afternoon and evening before bedtime.
- Help your child increase bladder capacity by getting him or her to wait as long as possible before urinating during the day.
- If you use terry nappies at night, double-nappy your child. For a larger child, you could try adult-sized disposable incontinence pads and International Disposable Corporation (UK) Limited will supply these by mail order. For more information write to them at Navigation Road, Diglis, Worcester WR5 3DE (Telephone: Worcester (0905) 356524).
- Help your child imagine, at bedtime, the possibility of a whole *dry* night — the power of positive thinking! You might wish to add the use of an incentive chart to turn thinking into visible progress.
- Assure your child that bedwetting for which there is no physical cause *will be* outgrown, *eventually*.

FIRST AID

The most carefully reared and watched child will sometimes be hurt . . . or uncomfortable . . . or sick. Knowing ahead of time what to do for minor things that don't require a doctor's immediate attention gives parents a sense of control that's comforting. A good first-aid booklet and one or two books on home medical care are recommended. (The first-aid booklet belongs in the bathroom, where you may need it in a hurry. Protect its cover with clear adhesive paper.)

Remaining calm yourself will help calm your child in a crisis. Remember that a good venting cry may be the best thing for a hurt child, female *or* male. When you think your child has cried long enough, tell him or her so. The idea is to teach the child that feelings should be expressed, but that there's also a time to regain control.

Handling 'ouches'

- Make pain time applause time. The whole family can gather to praise bravery under difficult conditions.
- Use a red or other dark-coloured flannel to clean a bloody wound; the blood won't show, and the child will be less scared. Likewise, keep red paper napkins on hand to blot blood before you wash.
- Pin an 'ouch' sign on clothes over a sensitive scraped area or injection to alert playmates to be careful. (But remember that children older than four or five may find it fun to *hit there*!)
- Help a child to stop crying by asking him or her to whistle. It's impossible to cry and whistle at the same time.
- Supply a 'pain bell' for a child to ring or a whistle for him or her to blow until the treatment has been completed.
- Get a child to count while an injection is being given to 'see how long it takes', just for distraction.
- Teach your child the relaxing and breathing techniques of prepared childbirth methods to lessen pain. Breathe in time together.

Bumps and bruises

Heat or cold . . . which should you use to keep swelling down and speed healing? Cold will help the bleeding under the skin that causes black and blue marks — but use it for only 24 hours after a bruise occurs. After that, heat, applied five or six times a day for the next few days, will speed recovery. Moderation is the key word — nothing too hot or too cold. Don't apply ice cubes directly onto tender skin (wrap them in a flannel) and don't use a high setting on an electric blanket.

- Keep a supply of ice lollies in the freezer for a tasty way to treat a bumped lip.
- Try putting the inside of a piece of banana skin on a bruise and cover it with a cool, wet cloth to prevent excessive discoloration. (Particularly good for a black eye — and far less expensive than the traditional steak!)
- Freeze wet flannels or water in freezer bags to apply to lumps, bumps or minor burns.

- Or freeze uncooked rice in a tightly closed plastic bag for a flexible compress.
- Use a can of frozen juice concentrate as a quick, non-drip frozen compress.

Bandaging

Probably no item in your first aid box is as 'magical' in its healing properties as a single plaster. And if one is good, several are even better.

- Let your child put a plaster on the same ouch-spot on a doll so that pain can be shared and thus lessened.
- Cover a chafed or scraped knee or elbow with the cut-off top of an old sock to give extra protection to the bandage underneath and yet allow for active movement. A variation of this protection is a towelling wristband.
- Make a lolly stick splint for an injured finger or slip a small plastic hair roller over the bad finger to protect it from painful knocks.
- Put ointment on the plaster — not the sore — when it is necessary to apply something that stings.
- Saturate a piece of cotton wool with baby oil and rub it over the adhesive part of the plaster so it comes off easily.

Splinters

- Get your equipment arranged before you start: a bright light, perhaps a magnifying glass, and tweezers or a sterile needle. (You can sterilize a needle by holding it in a flame for a few seconds.)
- Prepare the splinter area by soaking it in warm water or olive oil, or by covering it with a wet bandage or piece of adhesive tape for a few hours, or by holding the area over steam (from the mouth of a small bottle of boiling water). Any of these will loosen the splinter.
- Paint hard-to-find splinters with iodine; they'll show up as dark slivers.
- Numb the splinter area with ice or a little teething lotion.
- Ask your child to look the other way and sing a song, count

or tell a story while you prod gently at the splinter with the sterile needle.

- If you can't get a splinter out, leave it alone. Most splinters eventually work themselves to the surface. (For one that doesn't, you may want to see your doctor.)

Treating bites and stings

In addition to the many commercial products available, many simple household remedies work well.

- Rub a bar of wet soap over the bite, or apply toothpaste to it.
- Apply a paste of water and meat tenderizer. A paste of baking soda and water applied *immediately* to a bee or wasp sting reduces pain and swelling.
- Buy aloe gel at a health food store and apply this to the bite. (It's also good for sunburn.)
- Hold ice, or ice wrapped in a cloth, on the sting until it's numb.
- Crisscross the swollen area around a mosquito bite with a fingernail (on the grounds that one pain will cancel another) and apply some ever-available spit.
- Let an itchy child soak in a bath of water to which baking soda or laundry starch has been added. Or go to a swimming pool, just for the sake of getting into the soothing water.

Your Child Has an Insect in the Ear?
First try taking the child into a dark room and shining a torch just outside his or her ear. Insects are often attracted by the light and just crawl out. If that doesn't work, drip a few drops of rubbing alcohol into the ear to kill the insect, then ask the child to turn his or her ear down and the insect will probably drop out. Never try to get hold of an insect with tweezers or other instruments; you're apt to push the insect further in and there's a chance you could rupture the child's ear drum.

IN SICKNESS AND IN HEALTH

We experienced our parents' care when we were sick as children, but the job of caring for our own sick children seems awesome. As parents we act as nurses, comforters and companions to our sick children. Until your children can *tell* you what is bothering them, these roles can be especially difficult to play.

Many of the ideas in the section YOUR BABY'S DOCTOR apply to the care of toddlers and pre-school children as well as infants.

Taking temperatures

The rectal temperature is the most accurate. It will be one degree higher than an oral temperature. Other methods are possible for judging temperatures when you simply want to find out if a child is running a fever.

One way is to kiss your child's forehead (the temperature of your lips is more stable than that of your hands). The axillary (armpit) method is used by some parents. It's important to tell your doctor which method you have used when you phone him or her.

- Make inserting a rectal thermometer easier by smearing petroleum jelly on it.
- Give a child an egg timer or kitchen timer to watch while his or her temperature is being taken.
- Or let the child watch TV or listen to a record to shorten the wait.

Giving medicine

One of the hardest things about giving medicines to babies and small children is getting it *all down*. Don't try putting it in a bottle of formula or juice; you won't know how much the baby has received if all the liquid is not taken.

- Give a baby liquid medicine in a teat. (Wet the teat afterwards with a little water for the child to suck, to make sure all the medicine is taken.) Or use an eye-dropper or vitamin-dropper or a non-spill, graduated medicine spoon, which you can get from leading baby stores.
- Hold a paper cup under a child's chin when giving liquid medicine. Spills can be mixed with water or fruit juice and drunk from the cup.
- Coat a pill lightly with salad oil and it will go down easily. Or bury it in a spoon of jam.
- Or press the pill between two spoons to crush it, then mix it with honey or jam. Serve it by spoon with a drink of water or juice.
- Taste medicine yourself, and tell your child if it's not going to taste very nice. And if it isn't, rub an ice cube over the child's tastebuds on the tongue to kill the taste.
- If a child absolutely refuses medicine, with clamped jaws, gently squeeze his or her nostrils shut. The mouth will open quickly!

Constipation

Children are as variable in bowel movement patterns as they are in height and weight. Constipation is best treated by diet: encourage a child to drink lots of water and fruit juice (especially prune juice); give him or her high-fibre foods, such as bran cereal; give dried fruits as snacks. Always get advice from your doctor before treating a constipated baby. A doctor should be consulted if a child has great pain in passing stools or if blood appears in stools. Parents whose children sometimes have just a little difficulty have thought up ways to help.

- Spread a little petroleum jelly on the child's rectum or on a thermometer and insert into the child's rectum, as you would to take a temperature.
- Sit in the bathroom with your child. Little bottoms don't fit comfortably on adult toilet seats and moral and physical support helps.

- Help your child hold the 'cheeks' open to make passage easier.
- Ask your doctor for a relaxant medicine if you feel your child has an especially 'tight' rectum.

Diarrhoea

Diarrhoea can be caused by a number of serious illnesses or allergies; if it continues for several days, your doctor should be consulted. Most often, though, it's just a nuisance and a mess. One worry connected with long-lasting or serious diarrhoea is dehydration, for which a doctor should definitely be called. If your child is listless and lethargic and refuses liquids, suspect dehydration. Other symptoms are inability to retain liquids consumed, infrequent urination, dry mouth, few tears when the child cries, fever and dry skin. One test for dehydration is to pinch up a small fold of skin on the back of a child's hand. If it fails to sink back down when released, dehydration may be present.

- Encourage the child with diarrhoea to drink lots of clear liquids, including broth and carbonated drinks (let them stand for a few minutes or stir to remove bubbles), sugar water, but *not* milk. Give *only* liquids during severe diarrhoea.
- Or for a homemade 'binder' try water in which rice has been cooked.
- Don't give a commercial 'binding' product to a child under five or six without consulting your doctor.

> ***Phoning the Doctor***
> *Try not to have to hold a crying baby while you phone the doctor; neither you nor the doctor will be able to hear very well.*

Vomiting

- Give ice-chips instead of water to a child who can't keep liquids down. A child shouldn't drink after vomiting, but ice chips will help remove the bad taste.
- Place a plastic wastepaper bin on the floor next to the bed of a child who has been vomiting. An additional precaution is to have a plastic bowl and bath towel by the child's side.

- Or spread towels over the child's pillow and blanket; they are easier to take-off and wash than bed linen.

Colds and flu

- Use a soft old baby flannel or a man's large, soft handkerchief instead of a tissue to wipe a tender nose.
- Use an electric coffee maker with the lid off if a steamer or vaporizer isn't available when you need one. Make sure you put it where it can't be tipped over.
- Or run very hot water in the shower or bath and sit in the bathroom with the child, with the door closed.
- Hang a wet towel or sheet near a heater to increase the humidity in a room and make difficult breathing easier.
- Put a feverish child in a lukewarm bath and let him or her blow bubbles. When the child is bored with that give him or her an ice lolly to eat in the bath — fun, no mess, and the fever comes down.

Coughs and sore throats

- Lift up the head of the mattress to ease breathing for a child with croup or a bad cough by placing a folded blanket underneath it. Or raise the head of the bed with a few books under the bed legs.
- Make a cough medicine by mixing lemon juice and honey in equal parts. (Do not give honey to babies under one year old; there is some concern about its safety for infants.)
- Teach a child to gargle by doing it yourself while singing a song, letting the child join in.
- To help a child with croup, run hot water in the shower or bath and sit with the child in the steamy bathroom with the door closed.

Ear infections

- Eliminate or cut down the child's intake of dairy products to help reduce the mucus that contributes to ear infection.
- Lift up the head end of the mattress to help fluid drain.
- If you are worried about using a big ear dropper for oil your

doctor prescribes, try warming the oil in the small glass vial from a home pregnancy test kit and applying it with the small dropper from the kit. If you can do it while the child is asleep, so much the better.

Sickroom logistics

- Keep medicines, paper cups and other sickroom supplies in a container such as a shoe box or bread bin to save running from room to room.
- Or use a kitchen utensil stand for easy access to bedside supplies.
- Anchor a shoe bag between the mattress and base of the bed. The pockets, hanging down over the edge, will hold tissues and other small necessities.
- Pin a paper bag to the side of the mattress for soiled tissues and other rubbish.
- Keep a bell or whistle near a child's bed so he or she can call

for help when it's needed. (But tell the child to ring or blow just once or twice — not continuously!)

- Remember that your child may sometimes ask for a drink just to get your attention, but if it doesn't happen too often, go along with it.
- Make a table over a child's bed by using an adjustable ironing board, a picnic table with two legs folded up or a big cardboard box cut to fit over the child's legs.
- Let a sick child lie on an adjustable garden lounger. It allows for a variety of positions and saves continual propping up.
- Use a parent's old T-shirt as a sick gown for a child with chicken pox, a rash, or any eruptions that require lotion. The shirt won't rub and the lotion won't stain bedding or furniture.
- Serve meals on trays with a damp flannel or paper towel under the dishes to prevent them from slipping. The towel can be used to clean the patient's hands after eating.
- Cover the top blanket with a sheet that can be changed if food or liquid is spilt on it.

Casts on arms and legs

- Keep a plaster leg or arm cast dry for showering or bathing by covering it with a large plastic bag held in place with waterproof electrical or PVC tape.
- Smear petroleum jelly onto the edges of a cast to stop it chafing the skin.
- Sprinkle baby powder at the opening of a cast and blow it in with a hair dryer or vacuum cleaner (with airflow reversed) to relieve itching.
- Clean a dirty cast, if you have to, with white shoe polish.
- Make jeans and trousers usable over a leg cast by inserting a long zipper in the inside seam. When the cast comes off, the zipper can be removed and the seam sewn up.
- Use a solution of three tablespoons of vinegar to a quart of warm water to soak off casts that have to be changed regularly. After soaking, use bandage scissors to begin unravelling the gauze.

Chapter Four

Coping with Children at Home

The better organized a household is, the more smoothly it usually runs, but with children around, there's plenty of just plain *coping* with one situation at a time. Nevertheless, there are things you can do to help you cope better.

CHILD-PROOFING YOUR HOME

Obviously there's no way you can make your house 100 per cent child-proof, but, to start with, get down on your hands and knees on the floor. Crawl around where your child does (or will — you'll need to child-proof *before* he or she starts moving) and grab and pull on everything within your reach.

You'll find things that are easy to swallow, sharp edges underneath furniture and lots of things that will break off or fall over. Remember, too, that when you're visiting other people, you are responsible for child-proofing and keeping an eye on your child.

The kitchen stove

- Turn all saucepan handles to the back of the stove.
- Remove knobs, if you can, or tape them so they can't be turned on by children.
- Back a chair up to the stove for a young helper and let him or

her stand or kneel on it. The chair back provides a 'barrier'. (You must be there too, of course.)

- Let children stir food on the stove with long-handled wooden spoons; wood doesn't transmit heat.
- Always set a timer when you're cooking with children around. Children are distracting, and you can easily forget and start a fire or spoil food.

Around the kitchen

- Tuck leads safely behind kitchen appliances so children can't pull the appliances down on top of themselves.
- Use safety catches on drawers and cupboards. These are available from Mothercare and Babyboots stores. Or you can put a metal rule through some types of drawer and cupboard handles, or use metal shower rings or blanket pins at least for a few months.
- Use wet paper towelling or paper napkins to pick up small pieces of broken glass the broom misses so young crawlers won't cut hands and knees.
- Let children use plastic or paper cups instead of breakable glasses and china mugs.
- Store plastic cups in a drawer rather than in a cupboard. For the child who's able to reach the taps with a stool, they'll be easier to get.

- Move all cleaning materials from the cupboard under the sink (store plastic containers and pans the children can play with there instead) and *lock them up*. Paint the tops of dangerous materials with red nail polish and teach children that *red* means *danger*.
- Beware of a child tasting detergent from the dispenser in the dishwasher; add it only when you're ready to start the machine.
- Prevent toes being crushed by keeping shoes on a child who will be pulling tins or heavy objects out of a kitchen cupboard.
- Don't use tablecloths until your child in the highchair is past the grabbing stage.
- Make loops of strong shoelaces and attach them to the back of the highchair and run a belt through them to stop your child climbing out.

The bathroom

The potential for poisoning in the bathroom is perhaps even greater than in the kitchen. A locking medicine cabinet is well worth the inconvenience it causes adults. Cleaning supplies, as well as medicines, must be locked up or put out of reach. Consider moving all medicines and cleaning products to a high cupboard in the kitchen where they'll be safer and where children are likely to be more carefully supervised.

While toilet paper can't be considered dangerous, remember that for about a year 'flushing fascination' may cause waste and might perhaps block the loo. Many parents keep toilet rolls off the holder during this period or discourage waste by keeping a rubber band around the roll.

- Replace child-proof caps on medicine carefully and promptly after use. Save caps you've finished with; often they'll fit on other bottles or jars you want to stop children opening.
- Keep the bathroom out of bounds for a small child by putting a bolt high up on the outside of the door.
- Hang a towel over the top of the bathroom door to stop children shutting it tightly and locking themselves in. Or stick tape across the doorknob bolt so it won't slip into the door jamb.

- And, outside the door, keep the key or a tool with which you can unlock it.
- Remove the bathroom doorknob altogether if it's one that doesn't unlock from the outside and you don't want to fit another.
- To prevent falls in the bath, use a bath safety mat.
- Use plastic or paper drinking cups rather than breakable glass ones.
- Take the phone off the hook while you are bathing your child so you won't be tempted to leave him or her alone in the bath if it rings.

The children's rooms

- Check regularly for loose eyes on stuffed toys and for parts of other toys that might come off.
- Throw away broken toys, for safety's sake.
- Use open, stackable boxes or a vegetable rack for storing clothes so that a child can see and reach them easily without the possibility of pulling a drawer out on top of himself or herself.
- Use a rawlplug and screw your child's desk or bookcase to the wall to stop the child climbing up and tipping them over.
- Glue suction pads or small blocks of cork onto the undersides of the corners of a toy chest lid to avoid fingers being crushed. Or install a pneumatic door spring to make the lid open more easily and close slowly. Better still, keep toys behind sliding doors or on open shelving.

- Don't place a cot or other furniture that can be climbed on near a window.

Moving into the big bed

- Let your child start using a pillow while still in the cot — it will help him or her learn to 'centre' the body while asleep.
- Lower the side of the cot and put a stool beside it for a young walker who is about to go into a big bed. It's better to help your child climb out safely than to risk a fall.
- Push one side of the big bed against the wall for a child who's just moved into a big bed. Put a cot mattress on the other side to cushion an accidental fall. Or use a removable guard rail on that side for a few weeks.
- Turn the blanket crosswise, allowing for extra tuck-in along the mattress length.
- Roll up two blankets and put one under each side of the mattress, lengthwise, to make a small 'valley' for the child to sleep in.

If a Product Causes Injury...
If something you buy causes injury to your child and you wish to make a complaint, or if you are concerned about the safety of a piece of equipment or furniture, you can get help and advice from your local Trading Standards or Consumer Protection Department, Consumer Advice Centre or Citizens Advice Bureau. Their addresses will probably be in your local phone book, otherwise ask at your council offices.

Doors and windows

- Child-proof windows with gratings or a screen. Or you can buy a fitting that allows windows to open only a few inches or one that allows windows to be locked in any open position.
- Open windows at the top if possible.
- Put transfers at child's eye level on sliding glass doors as a reminder that they *are* glass, not open space.
- Attach a bell to a door that a small child can open to warn you if he or she wanders out.

- Fasten an old sock over the doorknob with a rubber band. Adults can squeeze hard enough to turn the knob; small children can't.
- Put bolts high up on the outsides of doors to older children's rooms or other rooms you don't want toddlers to go into. (Caution: children can be locked *in*, also by older children who are 'just playing' or by lazy baby sitters.) Use the bolts also on outside doors, but of course they'll only work in wood, so choose a wooden door instead of a metal one if you have the option and want to do this.
- Attach a flat curtain rod at child's height to a door that you want a child to be able to push open.

Stairs

- Put up a safety gate at the top of the stairs; it can be secured when little ones are on the loose and taken away at other times.
- Teach toddlers to crawl downstairs backwards and to get down from furniture backwards.
- Attach a rope to the lower post of the stair bannisters so there'll be something for your child to hang on to if he or she wants to climb up.

Electricity

- You can simply make sure that furniture is placed in front of every electrical socket in your home, but it's better to cover the sockets themselves. To begin with, cover them with strong, clear tape. When your child tries to remove it, fit socket safety covers which are available from Mothercare and Babyboots stores.
- Wind up excess lengths of plugged-in leads and fasten with rubber bands or freezer bag ties to stop your child sucking or chewing them and risking getting a bad mouth burn.
- Tape electricity wires to walls to prevent tripping over them.

All around the house

- Don't assume that squeezing books tightly into a bookcase will stop a determined toddler pulling them out. Chances are the bookcase will topple over before the child gives up.

- Leave lower bookcase shelves and the shelf under the television stand free for toys and children's books — your possessions can be returned to their proper places in a few years.
- Cover the rods used for handles and pedals of rocking horses with the kind of rubber tips you use on walking sticks to make them less dangerous. Or use plastic bike handles with formed grips.
- Apply a foam rubber strip with adhesive backing (used for insulation) to the frame of a baby's walker to protect your furniture. The foam sticks to itself, so can be wrapped around twice.
- Turn a desk with its drawers to the wall — use only the surface.
- Glue small cork blocks or suction pads to each end of the piano keyboard lid to prevent fingers being crushed.
- Pull chairs up close to the dining table so that a toddler can't climb up on them.
- Pick up your toddler and take him or her with you when you leave a room to answer the phone or the doorbell; it takes only a minute for a child to get into trouble.
- Or at least put the baby in the bouncing cradle *inside* the playpen if you have to leave a baby and a toddler in a room alone together. Or put the toddler in the playpen.
- And put the Christmas tree inside the playpen to keep it out of a toddler's reach.
- *Don't ever* let a child run with a lolly stick, or any similar object, in his or her mouth.
- *Never* leave a plastic bag where a child can play with it — suffocation can result. And when you throw a plastic bag away, be doubly safe and tie knots in it.
- Hold down the receiver buttons on the phone with a wide rubber band so that if your child takes the receiver off, your line won't become 'unobtainable'. Also he won't be able to make calls accidentally.
- Hang the phone wire on a cup hook screwed into the wall above the phone so your child can't pull on it.

Preventing Accidental Poisoning

The most common causes of poisoning in children of six and under are, in order, drugs, plants, personal care products and household cleaners. Children should be supervised especially carefully before meal times — they're more liable to sample foreign substances when they're hungry. Teach your child to say 'ahh', at an early age; you may get a chance to see what's in his or her mouth and pull it out before any harm is done. Careful parents keep the number of their doctor by the phone. Always contact your doctor for advice *immediately* if you think your child has swallowed something poisonous. Or, better still, if there is a hospital nearby take your child there straightaway.

SAFETY OUTSIDE

A whole new set of hazards presents itself to a child outdoors and away from home. There are attractive things to taste, unfamiliar settings to investigate, interesting equipment to experiment with and dangerous streets to cross. There's often also a possibility of getting lost.

You might consider attaching a large side-view mirror to an appropriate spot outside your kitchen window to keep a play area in your line of sight, when children begin to play outside alone.

In the garden

- Glue a rubber bathmat onto a swing seat to stop your child slipping off.
- Don't use ordinary clothesline for ropes for a homemade swing; it's not strong enough. Nylon, sisal or polyethylene ropes are better.
- Cover swing chains with sections of garden hose to avoid clothes getting torn and to give a more comfortable grip.
- Wrap adhesive or electrical tape round the hose on swing chains to show the child where he or she should hold on to get the correct balance.
- Spead four to six inches of loose material such as sand, shredded tyres or pieces of foam under swings and other playground equipment to cushion falls.
- Cover exposed screws and bolts with caps or tape: pinch

the ends of S-hooks together with pliers so they can't catch a child's skin or clothing.

- Check your own outdoor equipment for safety regularly and also check playground equipment at your local park, or any other your child might use.
- Place a ladder across the driveway a few feet from the end to stop pre-schoolchildren riding bikes into the street. Or paint a red stripe across the driveway as a reminder.
- Don't buy plastic riding toys which have seams going round the wheels — the seams will eventually split and a nasty fall could result.

In the car

There is *no safe alternative* to an approved, reliable car restraint — a car seat for a baby or small child under about 40 pounds or four years old, or a seat belt for an older child. Parents who may be tempted to transport a baby in a wicker crib or unrestrained carry cot and to let older children romp about in the back of an estate car must be warned that they're tempting fate. Children usually accept safety habits well if they are established right from the start and *never* varied. To protect your car upholstery, put a strip of vinyl carpet protector under the child's car seat.

- Teach children a car safety routine: an adults says, 'Hands up — doors closed and locked. Fasten belts. Blast off!' An older child can be appointed 'First Mate' to see that the procedure is carried out correctly.
- Choose a car seat that lets a toddler sit high enough to see out of the window.
- Pull over to the side of the road if there's screaming or fighting in the car. Stay there until everyone settles down.
- Spread a light-coloured sheet, towel or blanket over a car seat in the summer to avoid a 'hot seat' that can cause second-degree burns to a child's tender skin. When the child is old enough to use a seat belt, keep a towel in the car for the same purpose.
- Put a hat on a small child to shield his or her eyes from the sun in the car. Or glue strips of Velcro above side windows, sew Velcro to one edge of a towel and attach it to cover the window where the sun is coming in. Or apply 'solar film' to the window on the side of the car where you put the seat.
- Carry any sharp or heavy object in the boot, not in the passenger area.
- Never let a child play with the controls of a car; get a play steering wheel for one who loves pretending to drive.
- Never leave children unattended in a car and don't leave the car motor running when childen are playing near the car.

GETTING CHORES DONE

B.C. (Before Children), when you could do housework without interruption, you may have had the best-kept house around. That's not possible with little children around. 'A clean house shows a life misspent' is a slogan you may wish to adopt.

Keeping children out of the way

You can try to do housework 'around' your children, stopping when you have to and getting on when you can. Or you can let them help you (remember that sometimes they're really learning!). Or if you want them out of the way altogether, see if they can go to a friend's house to play or ask a grandparent to take them out. The cardinal rule for many parents is that children's nap-times and bedtimes are *not* signals for them to start work — they're for relaxation and enjoyment.

- Put your baby in a padded laundry basket or small cardboard box with a few toys and take him or her with you from room to room as you work. It's a good way for a baby to practise sitting for short periods of time.
- Let the parent who's not doing the housework take over the child entertaining.
- Put the baby in a backpack. He or she will be in the desired place (near you), and your hands will be free to work.
- Give your child his or her own kitchen drawer or cupboard stocked with assorted plastic containers, cans and other safe kitchen items.
- Allow your child to play with water in the sink while you work in the kitchen — but do it on the day you plan to wash the floor!

- Give a small child a short piece of sellotape or masking tape to play with if you want a few quiet minutes to work or talk on the phone. Or put a dab of baby lotion on the highchair tray to keep your child busy.
- Curb a child's impatience for 'the cake to be done' or 'playtime with Mum' to come by setting a timer and letting him or her watch it go round.
- Hang a mirror on the wall in the kitchen so that you can see childen in the next room. (This lends credence to the 'eyes-in-the-back-of-the-head' myth.)

Encouraging tidiness

- Keep a clean new dustpan in the toy box. A child can scoop up small objects with it. Or let the child gather up toys with a rug rake.
- Make a child who gets pocket money pay you a penny for every toy or article of clothing you pick up. Keep them in a big bag or box until you've been paid. Or ask him or her to do a special chore to get a toy back.
- Or let anything you do pick up simply *disappear* for a time.
- Offer to pick up your child's toys occasionally, in return for him or her doing one of your simpler chores.
- Try helping your child sometimes; it's more fun to work with company than alone.
- Encourage tidying up as soon as an activity has finished instead of at the end of the day to make the task less overwhelming.
- Ask visiting friends to help with tidying up before they leave.
- Help the children put their things away on open shelving by drawing labels for items and taping them on the shelves.
- Fix a basket ball ring over a child's laundry basket to provide an incentive for throwing in dirty clothes.
- Put a tall, narrow, plastic container in each child's wardrobe for them to put their dirty clothes in, or hang a colourful pillowcase, with loops sewn onto it, on the back

of the door for dirty washing.

- Set an example of tidiness for your child to follow by putting your things away, too.

Children actually helping

Even very small children can help around the house, if you're patient and don't expect perfection. It's important to remember to stress the importance of *all* work, to express appreciation for any job well done and to switch jobs occasionally to avoid boredom. If you're cheerful when you're working and try to find some humour in humdrum activities, the children will probably follow suit. Rewards inspire help, too, and good workers may occasionally have a treat. Just remember to make it a firm rule *never* to redo work a child (or your partner!) has done. Willing help will be hard to come by if you do.

- Give a child a card with a smiling face on it, or another token, to put in a place where he or she has done a chore or favour without being asked. Then make sure you notice the card and praise the child.

- Put a time limit on chores, or time them with a timer or a record on the stereo, to make work seem to have an end. Or have a race to see who can finish a job first if it isn't really important how well the job is done.

- Try printing titles of jobs on slips of paper when there's a lot to do and you want everyone to help. Include some that say 'Hop on one foot' and 'Eat a biscuit'. For little children you can draw pictures to illustrate such jobs as 'Feed the dog' and 'Lay the table'.

- Give a reason for tidying up and set a deadline: 'before Daddy comes home' or 'by lunch-time'. Not having to 'do it now' gives a child a choice and makes a job seem to be something he or she wants to do.

- Let the smallest child pick things up and give them to you or to an older child to put away, when everyone is helping to tidy up.

- Give each child a specific number of things to pick up, and count them as the job gets done. Or ask the child to pick up things beginning with letters you call out or which are the colours you say.

GETTING ORGANIZED

Saving time, money and trouble is something most parents want to do. To find a clever use for an item that's no longer needed for its original purpose — to protect a piece of furniture so that it outlasts its expected lifetime; to make a child's room a haven of comfort and convenience at little or no cost — all can give a feeling of achievement.

Something out of something else

- Use metal shower curtain rings as locks for garden gates.
- Use a baby's outgrown plastic bath for water play outdoors or indoors, with a big plastic tablecloth under it. Or use it as a portable toy box, indoors or out.
- Carpet playpen floors with new carpet scraps or samples, for comfort and warmth, or with vinyl scraps or samples to make it easy to clean.
- Moisture-proof a vinyl playpen pad by covering it with a piece of quilted material or with a length of towelling.
- Mend a torn mesh playpen with dental floss or fishing line.
- Turn an old piano stool into a play table for children to sit at on low chairs (storage tins or buckets turned upside down are fine). It even offers storage space.
- Cut away part of the front and sides of a medium-sized plastic wastebasket, smooth the edges carefully and put a large pillow in the bottom for a bucket-type seat.
- Spread out an old window blind on the carpet to cover the floor where children are playing or colouring. A fabric backed vinyl tablecloth works as well.
- Use a large old nappy pail as a laundry basket.

Children's rooms: walls

- Paint a growth chart on the wall for a visible, long-lasting record.
- Cut pictures appropriate to a child's age and interests from self-adhesive vinyl. Press them onto a painted wall for economical 'wallpaper'.

- Cover a section of a wall with shelf paper for drawing or paint a wall or door with blackboard paint for a child to scribble on. Use a big old powder puff for an eraser. If crayon marks get onto a painted wall, remove them with toothpaste on a damp cloth.
- Or put plain oilcloth on the wall with drawing pins. It can be used as a blackboard, it wipes clean and can be easily replaced when worn out. Childen love to draw and paint on artists' canvas, too, but it can't be washed clean.
- Make a notice board from the side of a really large box. Trim neatly and put colourful masking tape round the edges for a border.
- Put cork squares on the inside of the bedroom door — they serve the double purpose of muffling noise and providing a board to pin things on.

Children's rooms: furnishings

- Avoid shag pile rugs — dangerous objects, as well as food and plasticine, can be hidden in the pile. A low-pile, washable bathroom rug is practical for a small child's room.
- Consider installing track lighting and avoid the problems of table lamps which can be knocked over.
- Hang a discarded lamp shade from a ceiling light fixture

and attach small, no-longer-played-with toys with fine wire or fishing line.

- Avoid bunk beds, at least until your child is dry all night. It's hard to change linen on both upper and lower bunks. You might like to encourage the use of sleeping bags instead of sheets and blankets if you *do* have bunk beds. At least get fitted top sheets as well as bottom ones, if you can find them, or make them if they're not available.
- Speed up bunk bed-making by making fitted bedspreads out of ordinary ones. It saves all the tucking-in and you can use the spare material for cushion covers.
- Turn an old single bed or cot mattress into an extra bed for friends staying the night. It slides under a bed for storage.
- Use bean-bag chairs in children's rooms, or big foam pillows that can be used for building material as well as for sitting and tumbling on. It's a good idea to ban shoes in the bean-bag chair — a tear can be disastrous.
- Make more space for play, and make the room look bigger, by removing the fitted cupboard door and putting the child's desk inside the cupboard.

STORING STUFF

The number of things a child accumulates seems to be in direct proportion to his or her age. The new baby's clothes and toys take up a lot of space, the toddler's even more. But, oh, the pre-schoolchild's stuff! It's worth spending a little more time and effort on organization, especially if you want to encourage your child to be responsible for his or her own belongings.

Children's clothes

- Store small children's socks in small plastic containers which have been carefully washed and put into drawers.
- Store underclothes, socks, T-shirts and other small items of clothing in stackable plastic boxes that are open on the front. They're easier for children to use than heavy drawers.
- Cut out pictures of clothing items and stick them on the appropriate drawers to help children find and put away their clothes.

Hanging cupboards

- Make cupboard lights easy to turn on by tying brightly coloured cotton reels to the pull-chains or cords.
- Make a clothes rail at child's height by suspending a broom handle from the normal rail with strong cord at each end. The cord can be shortened to lift the rail up as the child grows.
- Give each person a coat hook and put a wicker bicycle basket over each to hold hats, gloves and scarves.
- Or attach a shoe rack or cloth shoe bag to the inside of the cupboard or on the wall next to it.
- Put a clothes hook low down on the back of a child's bedroom door for pyjamas and dressing gown.
- Hang your buggy on a hook in a cupboard to keep it out of the way, or put it in your umbrella stand or a tall basket near the front door.

Children's toys

Of course the trick is to accumulate the minimum – especially of toys with a million pieces. What you don't have . . . you don't have to store. How simple it sounds!

- Remember that horizontal storage is better than vertical for toys; small items get lost and sometimes broken at the bottom of big chests or boxes.

- Build shelves with bricks and boards, but not so high that there's a danger of them toppling over. The area underneath makes a good 'garage' for pull toys and cars and the shelves can be used for books and toys.
- Put up a wooden pole with pegs in it from floor to ceiling. Sew loops on stuffed animals and hang them on the pegs. It keeps them tidy and looks decorative, too.
- Or attach inexpensive netting in folds to the wall to give each stuffed animal its own 'cage'.
- Hinge a wooden stair step and put a floor under the step to give you a nice little cupboard for toys or boots.
- Attach strips of Velcro horizontally on walls at your child's height and sew or glue other strips on toys. The child 'sticks' his or her toys away.
- Store a few toys in a plastic clothes basket, which even a small child can easily pull from room to room for playing with and for picking things up quickly. (And when your child no longer uses it, you can use it.)
- A number of objects make good toy tidies. Among them are:
  A small suitcase.
  A freezer basket.
  The old wicker crib.
  Laundry bags, hung from wall hooks.
  Large, clear boxes.
  Baskets, attached to the wall.
  Fishing tackle boxes.
  Pedal bin.
  Stackable plastic vegetable trays.
  A plastic dish drainer (for books and records; the cutlery section will hold pencils and crayons).
  Three, five or seven 4 litre plastic ice cream cartons, glued together with open ends facing the same way, and spray painted. Set the assembly on its side, like a wine rack, to hold small toys or painting materials.
  A plastic rubbish bin with a swing lid.
  Large ice cream containers.
  Large heavy boxes cut down and covered with adhesive paper or wallpaper.
  Disposable nappy boxes.

Chapter Five

The Challenge of Parenting

Perhaps the greatest challenge of parenting is to help our children become social human beings. We want them to become secure, competent, well-adjusted, polite, and independent human beings, but those qualities can't be developed by simply following a formula. Our children's unique personalities and our own, plus all the other factors in our particular situations, combine to further complicate the already complicated process of growing up.

MANNERS

Setting a good example in social situations is important. 'Don't do as I do, do as I say' doesn't wash, even with little children. In order to cut down on the use of 'No' in front of others (and alone at home, too,) some parents try to say 'Yes', with conditions. 'Yes, you may have a biscuit — after dinner.' 'Yes, you may play outside — after you've had a sleep.'

Being quiet

- Choose front-row seats at church services or other gatherings where children are apt to be noisy or fidgety. Knowing they can be seen helps some behave well, and most enjoy being able to see what's going on.
- Or sit at the back where you can make a quick exit if necessary. Some people say you should only leave when it's

absolutely necessary and should return as soon as the child has used the potty or when the screaming has stopped.

- Sit a child between two adults at a meeting or service.
- Teach your child to whisper — a technique that must be learned — before you take him or her to places where talking aloud isn't possible. There's 'outside' and 'inside' talking, too — loud and soft.
- Find little things for children to do when they must be quiet in church or at meetings. They could keep track of how many times the rabbi or minister says 'God', or they could count the number of children in each row of seats.
- Take an assortment of quiet toys or objects in a small bag for a child to play with at a meeting or service and let him or her carry them. One possibility is a pile of fabric scraps pinned together. Or take a spool of thread and break off short lengths for your child to play with, as long as he or she is old enough not to try to eat them.
- If you want to take a 'quiet food', try raisins.

Table talk

- Teach children to modulate their voices by recording them on tape and playing it back so they can hear their own stridency.
- Set up a series of signals to correct table manners. Quietly saying, 'Twenty-two', for example is not annoying to children and makes correcting them when you are out less obvious. (But some parents say doing this leads to a game for older children, who sometimes enjoy putting their parents through a little exercise in calling numbers.)

The proper response

- Refuse to respond to 'what?' once you've explained 'pardon?' Wait for 'please', 'thank you' and 'excuse me' until they're second nature.
- Don't let go of something you're offering your child until you hear 'please' or 'thank you'.
- Apologize for your own lapses and ask children to do the same.

Telephone interruptions

You can keep your phone calls to the minimum while your child is in the interrupting stage; you can have little talks about manners; you can walk about, keeping order while you're talking, holding an extra long phone lead above your head. But the interruptions probably won't really stop until your child is old enough to make and receive calls and realizes the importance of being quiet while someone's on the phone. In the meantime, there are things to try.

- Take advantage of the time to hold and cuddle your child.
- Allow water play in the sink, if you're talking in the kitchen and can keep an eye on the child.
- Keep a special box of toys or a pad of paper and a few crayons near the phone, to be played with only while you're talking.
- Get your child a toy phone to use while you're on *your* phone.
- Teach your child to put his or her hand up or to put it on his or her head if it's really necessary to interrupt you. You can

finish your conversation or ask the caller to hold on for a moment while you see to the child.

- Try to teach your child to know you must not be interrupted. Stand up for uninterruptible calls; sit down for calls when it won't matter.
- Sometimes (you'll be sorry if you allow it to become a habit) let the child say hello to your caller, if it's someone like Grandma, who won't mind.
- If your child has a set sleeping time during the day, try to make your calls then, and ask callers to ring you back at that time.

TANTRUMS

Most parents believe it's best to ignore tantrums whenever possible, because when there's no audience, there's no need to perform. Many warn, though, that it's important not to ignore the *child*. They wonder if they're being too strict, holding too high expectations or perhaps simply not giving enough affection. Try, too, to avoid a tantrum: don't let your child get overtired or frustrated. Giving a little help with a toy that won't work, insisting on a short rest or offering a small snack — any of these may avert the tantrum if you can see it coming.

Dealing with temper tantrums

- Let your child scream to his or her heart's content sometimes (outdoors, perhaps, if you live in the country). Everybody needs to let off steam occasionally.
- If your discipline precipitated the tantrum, tell the child firmly that the rule still stands and that he or she will have to deal with the tantrum alone; then ignore the child.
- Try to distract the child by doing or saying something unusually silly. You might even stage your own mock tantrum. Or switch the light off and on rapidly, another attention-getter. Some parents suggest pouring a glass of water over a child's head for *real* drama.
- Disappear! If you're in another room, you'll feel better, and the tantrum will probably be short-lived. If the child follows you, move again.

- Stop breath-holding during a tantrum, if it continues and you're worried about cyanosis (lack of oxygen to the brain), by blowing gently into the child's face, splashing a small amount of cold water on the face or applying a cold cloth. Children usually do come out of this on their own.
- Take your child calmly to the car or a cloakroom if a tantrum begins when you're out. When the tantrum subsides, return to whatever you were doing. If you can't leave, simply let the tantrum continue and grit your teeth. Most of the adults who will see it have probably been parents of tantrum children, too.

Handling unacceptable behaviour

Behaviour you don't like is occurring. If it's something that's just irritating you or that's basically harmless to life and limb and furnishings, you may decide to ignore it and allow logical consequences to follow. If you're trying not to shout at your child, stand face to face with him or her and you'll find it virtually impossible to scream.

- Whisper, if it's noisy, and the child may stop to listen.
- Set a timer for when the behaviour must stop. Or start counting aloud, making sure the child knows how far you will count. And be prepared to do something at the end of the time: empty threats don't work.

- Call out a funny phrase, which is *always* your family secret signal to *stop*, whatever activity is going on. Remember to use it sometimes in positive situations, such as when crossing roads, and be prepared to have it said back to you.
- Congratulate your child on his or her control and good

sense when the misbehaviour stops.

- Set aside a place or chair where the child must stay if his or her behaviour gets out of hand and set a timer for three to five minutes. This not only stops the misbehaviour, it also gives the child a chance to calm down.

Calming an angry child

- Hold a small child tightly; rock and sing. Express your love in terms of increasing largeness: 'My love for you is as big as a flower . . . as big as a teacup . . . as big as a bush,' and try to get him or her involved in thinking up bigger and bigger things.
- Whisper in his or her ear. Screaming will usually stop, and if you can think of something really good to whisper, the child's mood may change.
- Tell your child there's a smile inside, and if it's not let out, it will turn to a giggle. It will, often. Or mimic your child, and exaggerate, and say, 'No laughing!' (This, of course, is ignoring the anger, so, when it's over, talk to your child about it.)
- 'Scold' a piece of furniture or a toy that causes trouble for your child. He or she will probably end up laughing.
- 'Lend' your child a hug and a kiss when things are going well and ask for the 'loan' to be repaid when anger strikes. This gives the child a chance to feel affection and calm down so you can talk about it.

Helping a child vent anger

Children, like adults, shouldn't be required to hold anger in. You may want to talk to your child about his or her anger, encouraging the use of words to express it, and showing your understanding. But remember that doing something physical may be more helpful for the child than anything else.

- Encourage your child to vent anger physically by running around outdoors, punching a big batch of play dough or hammering on a piece of wood.
- Teach the child to count to five in a *loud, angry* voice, to play an *angry* song on a musical instrument or to dance an *angry* dance.

- Or shout something loud with your child, and let your voices drop, drop, until there's silence.
- Ask an angry child to draw a picture showing how he or she feels, a creative way to relieve feelings.

SIBLING RIVALRY

The only real cure for rivalry is to have only one child; a certain amount of rivalry, jealousy and squabbling is normal between brothers and sisters. It's not possible to make anyone stop feeling certain emotions like hate and the need to win. Growing up knowing that there are times when you dislike someone you love is realistic and healthy.

It's usually best to let the children work things out for themselves, since a lot of fighting is done mainly to prod parents into doing *something*. Of course, there are times when you have to interfere for safety's sake — and others when you just can't stand any more fighting!

Fair is fair

- Make sure your children have rights to their *own* things. It's hard to share if they're not secure and guilt-free about ownership. Allow them *not* to share, if they wish.

- Don't label a child 'selfish' or show disapproval over unwillingness to share. Make a point yourself of sharing and make sure your children see you doing it.
- Tell a child who doesn't want to share, 'When you've finished, Dan can have it.' This lets the child know that someone's waiting, but eliminates the distress of giving up the toy immediately.
- Or set a timer to ring when it's time to exchange toys.
- Let one child cut the cake or divide the orange sections and the other have first pick when they're fighting about fairness.
- Or give each child a special day or days (like Monday, Wednesday, Friday) when he or she may make certain decisions, select menus, be first at everything.
- Play the 'stone game': put a small stone in one hand, and the child who picks the right one has first choice.
- Avoid fights over similar toys such as buckets and spades, balls and the like by choosing a colour for each child and always trying to buy those types of toys in the chosen colours.
- Divide a bedroom shared by squabblers with a bookcase and divide the cupboard by painting half one colour and the other half, another.

Changing the pace

- Suggest a new activity when the children are squabbling a lot. Boredom often leads to quarrels.
- Try to distract an older child if you can see that he or she is about to attack a younger one: 'Quick, I need you! Please come and help me.'
- Try spraying window cleaner on the inside and outside of a sliding glass door or downstairs windows. Put one angry child on each side with a dry cloth. By the time the glass is dry, the children will be laughing.
- Make the children hug each other when they fight. Next time they'll think twice — no one wants to hug a sibling he or she is angry with.

- End a verbal argument by getting the children to sing their complaints to each other.
- Ask the children for ideas to solve the problem. Let them think of special ways they can accommodate each other. Even if the ideas aren't workable, the children will be involved in sorting it out.
- Get up and go into the garden, if you can, or at least consider taking refuge in the bathroom. Like temper tantrums, fighting often stops when there's no audience.

End of options

- Send two quarrelling childen to different corners of the room and sit them down facing each other. They must stay there until they give each other 'permission' to leave. Negotiations usually lead to peace.
- Or ask each child to think of five things that he or she thinks are nice qualities or actions of the other. Mutual compliments often end the war.
- Force a compromise by removing the object of disagreement or separating the children.

BREAKING HABITS

Habits that parents don't like aren't necessarily bad ones — often they're just very annoying. Some are established as answers to frustration or anxiety, others as ways to relieve tension and give security in a confusing world. Some parents find that ignoring a habit helps, if no one is being hurt, but others try to get to the bottom of it. They make a chart, noting when and under what circumstances the habit takes place, then they try to avoid those situations arising or try and help the child cope with them.

Some parents try to distract the child, but they warn that this may only reinforce the habit if the child sees it as a way to get attention. Remember, anyway, that *you* can't break a child's habit — you can only help the *child* to break it.

The dummy

- Put vinegar or something else sour or bitter on the dummy — it won't taste nice.

- Lose the dummy of a child 18 months or older. At that age, he or she will probably understand the concept of losing things and won't question the fact that it's gone.
- Start a little hole in the dummy and enlarge it every few days until the 'taste' and shape are no longer appealing.
- Tell the child that when his 'last' dummy is lost or worn out, there will be no more. The advance warning may make giving it up easier.
- Try to coordinate giving up the dummy with giving up the usual nap, if it's possible. (But remember that if you get the child to give up the dummy the nap may go, too, whether you like it or not!) A very tired child will go to sleep quickly at night and probably won't miss the dummy much.

Biting

Children bite for different reasons, usually depending upon their ages. For a baby, biting may simply be a new tactile experience. The child who bites in anger or frustration usually outgrows the habit when he or she is old enough to talk about problems. Then, too, there is the possibilty that a child is imitating another biter — human or otherwise. Whatever the cause, vigilance is recommended until the habit is outgrown or 'cured'.

- Pinch the child's nose. He or she will release the victim.
- Remove the child from your lap or the room, explaining that biting is not acceptable.

- Say, 'No biting', perhaps while holding the child's jaw on either side of the mouth with thumb and index finger and applying light pressure.
- Dramatize your pain and sorrow; the child's sympathy may rise to the top. (If the child seems to think this is a marvellous game — try another tactic!)
- Try giving the child something he or she *can* bite, such as a rubber toy or soft doll. Or an apple or a crusty roll.
- Put the child's arm in his or her mouth and insist on a 'self-bite' to show how much it really hurts.
- Say, 'Oh, so you want to play the biting game!' and bite back gently.

Thumb-sucking

Many parents say, '*Don't try to stop it*; thumb-sucking fulfils a need for comfort and security.' Some dentists feel that, if it's continued for a long time, thumb-sucking or finger-sucking can change the shape of a child's mouth and put permanent teeth out of alignment — a good reason for regular dental check-ups. If you want to stop it, there are things you can try.

- Try giving a baby a dummy as a substitute.
- Try some physical means of stopping thumb-sucking, such as painting on a bad-tasting ointment that you can buy from a chemist. (Some parents warn, though, that if a child rubs his or her eyes, the ointment will make them sting.)
- Sew mitts to pyjama sleeves or buy or make finger puppets for the child to wear for sleeping.
- Put a kiss in each of your child's hands at bedtime and tell him or her to hold them closed all night to keep the kisses in.
- Restrict thumb-sucking for an older child to his or her own room. The desire can then be indulged, and you won't have to see it. The chances are that keeping you company in the rest of the house will become more important than the habit.
- Ask your dentist to warn the child about possible future dental problems, if he or she agrees that they may follow.

The voice of a 'neutral party' often carries more weight than that of a parent.

Dawdling

Dawdling is just a form of negativism, which most children pick up between the ages of two and three. Be patient — it passes.

- Set a timer in a child's room and make it a game for him or her to be washed and dressed by the time it goes off.
- Get your child an alarm clock to help instil a sense of responsibility about getting up. Be lavish with praise when responsibility is shown.
- Don't serve breakfast to a child still in pyjamas; one who's dressed before eating is ready to go out afterwards.
- Don't turn on the television until the child is dressed, in order to keep distractions to a minimum.
- Help your child to hurry by reminding him or her of the fun and exciting things that may happen during the day.
- Let a dawdler miss an activity, if it's possible to arrange it. The chances are the child will be ready the next time.

FEARS AND TEARS

The apparent fear that developing babies show by turning away from anyone other than a parent is nothing to apologize for or to worry about — it's a sign of expanding mental and emotional reaction. Toddlers and older children learn fear when they realize that there are some things they can't control. They may be afraid of being hurt or of pain, or being abandoned at bedtime or when left with a baby-sitter. Teasing and making fun of a frightened child may cause him or her to hide the fear behind belligerence or to give up and become withdrawn. It's important to *listen* carefully to a child to find out exactly what he or she is afraid of.

Facing up to fears

- If an eight- or nine-month old baby becomes frightened of the vacuum cleaner, carry the child with you as you vacuum; guide his or her hand to the on-off switch and let the child push with you.
- Do something physical about irrational fears of such things as 'monsters', say parents who think magical things can

only be dealt with magically. Spray them away with a spray can or perfume spray (the child will be able to smell the 'monster repellent' after you've gone); blow them out of the window; flush them down the toilet; throw them into the dustbin; get the family pet to come and eat them; or make up a spell to get rid of them before leaving the room. (Some parents disagree, though. They say that doing this reinforces the fear as the child thinks that the parent believes in them too. They feel it is better just to say 'There are no monsters, except in make-believe.')

- Treat all fears seriously, doing what you can to alleviate them. For example, if a child is afraid of shadows on the wall caused by traffic outside, take the trouble to move his or her bed to a 'safer' wall or to get opaque curtains.
- Go through the things that scare your child. Play 'what if', and discuss what your child should do if he or she gets lost, is in a car accident or if a parent is taken ill.
- Face up to fear. Admit that you — and all adults — feel afraid sometimes. Tell your child about fears you had as a child and how you overcame them. Or ask the child's grandparents to tell him or her about your fears.
- Don't discourage your child if he or she needs a 'security blanket' or another favourite object to feel safe.
- Don't let your child think the blanket or other object he or she becomes attached to is *bad*. Such security objects help ease the transition to independence and symbolize your child's ability to develop an interest in things outside himself or herself.
- Cut a favourite blanket in half and whisk the dirty half away for washing when he or she doesn't see you.

Fear of the dark

- Take a walk up and down your road at night in good weather to teach a child that the dark is magical, not spooky. Or lie on a blanket in your garden or the park, looking at the stars, watching for bats, listening to night sounds.
- Remember that there's no law that a child can't sleep with the light on. You can provide a nightlight easily by

replacing the bulb in a normal lamp with a small coloured bulb. Or consider a lighted fish tank that the child can watch until he or she falls asleep.

- Give the child a wind-up musical box; play a tape of soft music; or turn on a radio to distract him or her.

Nightmares

- Make sure a child who has had a bad dream or a nightmare is completely awake. Talk to him or her soothingly and reassuringly; wait for an answer that shows he or she is not still half asleep.
- Take the child to the toilet; it's probably a good idea anyway, and it will make sure the child is completely awake.
- Talk about the dream a little, explaining that it was *only* a dream and not reality. The next day, talk about it more and discuss the fact that dreams are marvellous experiences over which a person can have control. If something's chasing you, for example, you can turn around and chase *it*.

Fear of thunder

- Play records of marching music to cheer up a child afraid of a thunderstorm. The loudness of the music will drown out the thunder, and marching will give him or her something to do.

- Boom back at thunder.
- Or play a game, like seeing if you and the child can sing a whole verse of a song or recite the whole alphabet before the next clap of thunder.

Saying goodbye, with tears

There are parents who patiently accept the inconvenience of staying at home with a child until he or she feels completely happy about being left with a baby-sitter. Others say that you shouldn't feel guilty about going out — both parents and children are happier with occasional separations. They say that children are clever enough to sense your guilt and to play on it. Some parents sneak out while the child is occupied and others say, '*Never* do that!' Many try only to go out for a little while if they have a new baby-sitter.

- Get the sitter to come about half an hour before you have to leave so that an activity can be started before you go and the child will be busy.
- Spend a few minutes with the child before you leave, and try not to have to rush off hurriedly.
- Use a set goodbye ritual, including a hug and a kiss and such things as waving goodbye from the door or window or beeping the car horn as you pull away.
- Kiss the child's palm and close his or her fingers into a fist, explaining that, if there's a need for a kiss, there's one in there, ready and waiting.
- Keep family pictures handy so the sitter can look at them with your child. The child will feel secure about his or her background and 'belonging'.
- Try to be back when you've said you will be, and remind the child that you always come back. Phone if you're delayed and explain the problem to your child in person if he or she is old enough to talk on the phone.
- Tell a child who doesn't understand about time that you'll be back 'after lunch' instead of 'in three hours'. For a child who's a little older, set a clock with the time you'll be back so that he or she can compare it with one that's running.

- Leave your child at a sitter's house with a security blanket, book or favourite toy.
- Tell the child beforehand — some days before if possible — that you'll be going out. Say who will be looking after him or her and what exciting things they may do, but make sure you don't promise something that you haven't already arranged with the sitter.

DEVELOPING SELF-ESTEEM

Parents who want their children to develop high self-esteem make a point of treating them with respect and courtesy; they don't keep 'please', 'thank you' and 'I'm sorry' for adults. They say that they don't belittle their childen and that they correct or punish them in private, when they can, to help their children save face. And they say, 'Don't take it all too seriously — no single incident will shape your child's character.'

Showing respect

- Knock on your child's door if it's closed and wait to be asked to go in. Your child should return the courtesy to you.
- Borrow something belonging to your child only after you've asked, just as he or she must before borrowing something from you. If you borrow money, give the child an IOU to make the transaction 'legal'.
- Tell your child very clearly, when necessary, that it is his or her *behaviour* that is naughty or rude. Say, 'That's a bad way to behave' not 'You are a bad child.'
- Soften a criticism, when you have to criticize, by giving your child a compliment before and after it.
- Take the time to introduce your children to others, as you do adults.

Making children feel special

- Use your child's name often in conversation and use nicknames only if he or she really likes them. And use the name in other ways — wooden letters on the wall of the child's room, a sign on the door, a puzzle, a homemade place-mat.

- Make each child a *specialist* in the family — your 'favourite two-year-old', the 'exercise leader' or the 'nature lover'. (Some parents disagree with this suggestion and the next one, saying that other childen feel left out. Instead they suggest that parents praise children's actions and avoid using labels — even good ones.)
- Share a special secret with each child. It could be a code word that no one else knows. (Those who disagree with this suggestion try to plan one-to-one sessions with each child instead.)
- Tell your child stories in which he or she is the hero.
- Write about your child... with your child. Keep a joint diary, let the child draw illustrations, and cover the pages with clear adhesive paper to preserve them. Sometimes read one or two pages to the child at bedtime.
- Share baby record books and photo albums with children, so that they can enjoy their own growth and development.
- Keep a 'baby' drawer or box into which you drop an anecdotal record of your child's life several times a year and perhaps even a letter you wrote to the unborn child while you were pregnant. The drawer or box serves as a place to store the child's artwork as he or she grows older, and going through everything once or twice a year is fun for everyone.
- Tape-record your child's voice, as he or she sings, recites or just talks to you, and play it back with your child, expressing your delight again at his or her verbal skills.
- Let the children entertain you with plays they make up. Give a child a wooden spoon or a beater from a mixer for a 'microphone' and clap enthusiastically as they act it out.
- Surprise your child with a large, inexpensive enlargement of a favourite photo of himself or herself.

Special tips for fathers

In spite of the fact that *Dada* is one of the first words a baby learns (often inspired by *Mama*, who wants to make Dad feel good), fathers often spend comparatively little time with their children when they're small. Today more and more fathers are finding that they want to have a more meaningful influence on their children's lives and many have developed special things to do.

- Remember that physical contact with your child is important from infancy. Don't be afraid.
- Write down, periodically, your feelings about being a parent and about how you 'see' your child. You'll enjoy looking back over your writing, and so will your child when he or she is old enough.
- Shower or bath with your child when you come home from work or at bedtime, both to provide the child and yourself with pleasure and companionship and to give your spouse a little free time.
- Give your time, rather than things. Write out a list of activities you and your child enjoy sharing and let him or her choose one when a treat is called for.
- Remember to bring a souvenir home from each trip, if you travel, but it need not be an expensive present. The small soaps from hotels are always appreciated, as are airline magazines, plastic utensils from meals and packets of sugar or condiments.

Building self-esteem in the family

- Let each child do something alone with just one parent occasionally.
- Try to say at least one positive, encouraging thing to your child every day.
- Try to provide an alternative treat for a younger child if an older one has something special planned. For example, if the older one is invited to spend the night at a friend's house, a younger one might be allowed to sleep in the sibling's bed.
- Let even very young children participate in family meetings. Listen to them, and try to adopt their suggestions sometimes.
- Expect your children to do as much as they can, as well as they can, and let them know you do. But let them know that it's all right to make mistakes, too, and that mistakes — even Mum's and Dad's — show people ways to learn and improve.

Chapter Six

Family Heritage

Giving your child a sense of belonging to a special, important group — a family, large or small — is one of the nicest things you can do. One way of developing this sense is to help the child know all the members of the family and their relationships to one another — not always easy, the way some families are scattered today. Another is to observe family tradition. And then there's keeping track of it all . . .

BEING PART OF THE CLAN

Even when family members live nearby, children sometimes get confused about the relationships. Your efforts to give your child a sense of being a part of a clan will help give him or her a feeling of importance and a clearer self-image.

Understanding relationships

Who's who? Many families make it a point to discuss family relationships often: 'Grandma is my mummy; Uncle Roger is Daddy's brother.' And it's both instructive and fun to reminisce about family history and to talk about events currently going on.

- Put together a family of dolls or paper dolls to help a child understand relationships.
- Draw a family tree on shelf paper or paint one on a wall in

your child's room and stick on photos of relatives.

- Devise different names for children to call two sets of grandparents in order to distinguish between them — Grandma and Grandpa for one set, for example, and Nanny and Grandad for the other. Or add surnames. Some parents let the grandparents choose their own names.
- Use pictures to help acquaint children with relatives. Put together an album and look at it together often; give children photo cubes of their own. Or stick pictures on the refrigerator or on a board.

'Relative' activities

Nothing can quite replace visits for getting to know one's relatives; if your family is one that enjoys big get-togethers on holidays or occasional family reunions, your children are especially lucky. Imaginative use of the telephone, letters and the tape recorder can provide good substitutes for visits and gatherings, too.

- Let just one child at a time spend the night with grandparents if they live near you. The grandparents can serve a meal that the child especially likes, and the child can explore the grandparents' house and belongings and learn their routines.

- Give grandparents a photo album for pictures of their new grandchild and memorabilia such as first drawings. Ask them to write in the album about their memories. The visiting child will have his or her *own* book to look at over the years.
- Place photos of relatives near the phone so that childen can see the relative they're talking to. Or make a telephone book for your child, using pictures, instead of written names, of relatives (and friends) he or she is most likely to want to ring.
- Find the homes of relatives who live a long way away on a map. Do a little research on their cities or countries and ask them to send pictures of their homes, gardens and neighbourhoods.
- Or get a large jigsaw puzzle of Great Britain and let a child carry around with him or her the piece representing the county a relative lives in.
- Let the children send special drawings to grandparents and cousins. They'll probably get letters back, which will make those family members very special.

- Encourage grandparents who don't live near you to send notes, cards and inexpensive gifts by post, instead of phoning. Small children aren't usually able to carry on very interesting telephone conversations.
- Let your child add something to your letters to relatives — a scribble, a picture and, later, a full signature. You can take dictation from the child, too.
- Tape spoken 'letters' to relatives and post the tapes back and forth.
- Consider 'adopting' a grandparent if your child rarely sees any relatives. Perhaps you know of an older person near you who doesn't have any grandchildren and would like to take on this role.

TRADITIONS

Some traditions go back generations; others are begun when a new family is established and grows. A tradition can be as simple as the daily gathering at the dinner or breakfast table to share the day's events or as complex as a holiday celebration, including special menus and observances.

One thing to beware of is inflexibility in traditions. When one's outgrown, store it away in your memory and leave it there.

Birthdays

Some parents help small children keep track of the time before a birthday by describing it as so many 'sleeps' away or by making a paper chain with the child and letting him or her tear off a link each day. For the little child to whom a year is an eternity, consider having 'half birthdays', twice a year. And for one whose birthday falls near Christmas, choose (with his or her help) another day for the party and some birthday presents.

- Take your child out for lunch either to the child's favourite place or to a parent's place of work, if that's possible.
- Plant a tree, shrub or perennial plant that the child chooses as a lasting memory of every birthday.
- Give your child a gift each year to add to a collection you start for him or her in early childhood — coins, notes, thimbles, small cars, and so on.

- Write a birthday letter to your child each year, noting highlights of the year, changes in the family and the child, special accomplishments of the child. The letters will become valuable keepsakes for him or her later.
- Save the newspaper from the child's birthday each year to give him or her later.
- Ask the guests at the birthday party or family dinner to autograph the tablecloth with their names and the date; embroider the autographs or ask the writers to use coloured pens. Use the cloth each year, adding new names and repeating the old. Or ask guests to sign on a white bedsheet, and later make it into a quilt.
- Burn a big decorative candle each year at the birthday party for the number of minutes that corresponds to the child's age.
- Transfer all the notes you've made to the baby book and put the year's pictures into the album — and share your child's year with him or her. (Makes you get organized, too!)
- Select a dull month in which there are no family birthdays and have an *unbirthday* party every year, with *unbirthday* presents for all (*unwrapped*), an *unbirthday* cake, games and songs.

Gift-giving holidays

- Begin the gift-giving season by letting the children go through catalogues, marking items they like. You'll get an idea of the kinds of things they want.
- Make felt Christmas stockings for your children and add a new design each year, representing something important to your child for that year. Symbols can range from a scrap of a school play costume to a felt cut-out of an instrument the child has taken up.
- Take your children to a toy shop before gift-giving times and let them choose a toy to give to a less fortunate child, to teach them to enjoy giving as well as receiving.
- Get the children to wrap gifts in their own drawings.
- Use those extra pictures you accumulate of everyone in the family as gift tags.

- Give Grandma and Grandpa a toy of the children's choice on each gift-giving occasion. The toys remain at the grand-parents' home, to be played with only there — a permanent supply for visits.
- Give each child a Christmas tree ornament every year; store the ornaments separately and they'll make a treasured collection.
- Give your child certain types of gifts every year to make opening presents exciting: something to read, something to eat, something to play with outside, something snuggly to wear, something soft to take to bed. Or just three gifts (as Jesus received) — something special from Mum and Dad, something the child wants, and something he or she needs.
- Take a picture of your child playing with or wearing a gift he or she received from a relative or friend, and send it as a thank-you note to the person who gave it.

KEEPING RECORDS

The most important official record that parents must keep is their child's birth certificate. It's important to make sure the certificate is made out correctly and to keep it in a safe place, because you may need it when the child starts school, applies for a licence or passport, and so on. Many parents keep one certified copy in a bank safe deposit box and keep others at home for use as needed.

Other records are important for your child's medical history. And still others, in the form of diaries, tapes and photos, provide pleasant memories for a lifetime.

Medical and legal records

Some parents keep a notebook for each child, combining all medical, legal and school records. If advice and comments from doctors, dentists and teachers are included, the notebook can help to keep track of any recurring problems a child may have.

- Use the back of a copy of your child's birth certificate to record childhood diseases and their dates of occurrence.
- Or use recipe file cards for children's medical histories, noting illnesses, dates of vaccination and other information. The child can take the card on holiday or to

school, if at boarding school, and it can be kept as a permanent record throughout the child's life.

- Carry a recipe file card in your wallet for each child so that you'll have it to make notes on at the doctor's surgery; transfer the notes to the child's permanent records when you have time.

Written records for memories

- Use a calendar for a baby record book if you don't want to buy a special album.
- Keep a pad and pencil handy to note milestones reached by your children. They can be entered in the baby books when there's time, and you won't have to rely on your memory.
- Keep notebooks of your children's great sayings to read from when they're a little older and to give them when they're grown up.

Spoken records

Tape and cassette recorders are as common in many homes today as radios and TVs are. We may be hesitant to use a tape recorder at first — our voices sound so strange — but, with a little practice, it becomes a valuable recording tool. Children usually love recording straight away.

- Consider taping 'talks' that you have with your baby during feeding times. Go over the day's events and the baby's progress and accomplishments. Save the tapes for the child to listen to later on.
- Tape record all kinds of family events, from ordinary dinner table conversations to family conferences and celebrations.
- Let your child record a story he or she tells well, at various ages. The changes in voice and vocabulary will amaze you both, and you'll have a precious record of your child's voice, childhood delights and growth.

Records in pictures

Get good photos by moving in close to the child and by snapping quickly (babies and little children don't 'say cheese!').

Take lots of shots to assure yourself of getting some good ones. Keep backgrounds simple and uncluttered and get down to the child's eye level.

- Get a child to hold the family pet or a favourite toy if he or she is shy about having photographs taken.
- Twice a year take a picture of your child standing by a familiar piece of furniture or beside a parent whose hand rests on the child's head. Each half-year's growth shows up dramatically.
- Make photocopies of your child's hands from time to time.
- Trace your child's silhouette from a shadow every year or so.

Save Baby's First Shoes
Preserve them by filling them with plaster of Paris and later spraying them with gold, silver or bronze paint.

Chapter Seven

Families on the go

Today's families are part of a mobile society. They go out to work and play and shop, they go on holidays, and about 25 per cent of them move every year. Busy parents try to make each trip as enjoyable, convenient and safe as possible for themselves and the children.

ERRANDS

Start with a list of places you're going to and things you're going to do, to make your trip as efficient and as short as possible. Leave library books, shopping lists and anything else to be taken with you in a special place near the door, where you won't forget them.

Shopping with a small child — or with several — is not easy. Many parents try to shop alone for big grocery orders, leaving their children with friends or relatives. For older children, though, a trip to the supermarket can be a learning experience in both nutrition and economy.

Saving trouble

- Get yourself dressed first in cold weather so that your baby or toddler won't get too hot and irritable before you're ready to go out.
- Keep a few disposable nappies in your car glove compartment — just in case. And tuck a packaged

towelette and a plastic bag inside each, so that cleaning up and disposal are easy. Keep a box of nappies and towellettes at Grandma's, too, for unplanned visits.

- Hang some large safety pins on your keyring — you might need them for nappies or for pinning up clothing in an emergency.
- Change your baby in the boot of the car (with a blanket inside it) or in the back of a hatchback, instead of crouching uncomfortably on the back seat.
- Carry your child in a backpack while you're in the shops, but watch that your child doesn't start taking things off the shelves. If the child wants to walk, keep your hands free by putting your purse, nappy bag and anything you've bought in the backpack.
- Use an adult's belt as a shopping trolley 'safety belt' for a toddler to give both restraint and support.
- Take toys and a dummy with pieces of string or elastic tied to them, in your bag or pocket, and attach them securely to the shopping trolley. Stuffed toys can wear cheap cat collars with string leashes. (Try this on the highchair, too; your baby can 'fish' for toys.)
- Give the children something to eat as the sight of food seems to make them feel hungry. Take a snack or a picnic lunch or buy something nutritious to eat or drink.
- Keep a metal shower curtain ring on the nappy bag and attach it to the handle of the trolley or buggy to keep your hands free.
- Save shopping altogether, when you can, by catalogue shopping. You can compare prices in peace and quiet and save time, money and petrol. And children love to look through the catalogues, too.

Keeping tabs on children

- Don't attach your child's name to clothing in an obvious place, say some parents, as a lost child is likely to respond positively to anyone who knows his or her name — and some strangers are dangerous.
- Get an expandable identity bracelet for your child which states name, address and phone number, and make sure he

or she *always* wears it.

- Give your child a small flag to hold up if he or she gets lost.
- Buy two balloons — one for each hand — to stop a child grabbing and handling things.
- Dress a child who's not in a trolley in bright-coloured clothing (a red hat will do) to keep track of him or her.
- Have a special family whistle or tune children can recognize and use to find you if you get separated in a crowded place.

Involving the children in shopping

- Turn your child into a mini-shopper. Give him or her a handful of box tops or coupons from products to match up with products you intend to buy. Or make a grocery list in pictures for him or her to follow as you follow your own list.
- Take advantage of the opportunity to teach your child about nutrition, explaining why you buy some items and not others.

Going into town with children

- Put your baby's infant seat in the pram when he or she is old enough to sit up and take notice.
- Use a baby harness if your toddler is tired of the buggy. If you embroider it or sew on appliqués, it will look more personalized... less like a leash!
- If you go by bus, try and sit upstairs so the children will have a good view.
- On the bus or underground let the children try to 'guess' which stop is theirs so that they will learn their way around.
- Or, if they want to, let them sit a few seats away from you and pretend they are travelling alone. It makes them feel grown up, and they may pay more attention to the route.

Going to the Cinema?
Take your toddler's booster chair and put it in the cinema seat so he or she can see the screen without having to sit on your lap. It'll be more comfortable, too.

TRIPS

Adults may be able to throw a few things into a bag and dash off, but when the children are going too, things are different. It's easiest to travel with a child under six months — when he or she has long sleeps — but with older children, thoughtful advance planning pays off. It's usually best not to talk about a trip with children too far ahead in order to avoid unnecessary excitement. Try to arrange the timing of a trip so that everyone will arrive at the destination fresh and rested.

Packing

It's hard to travel light with children. Clothing, food and toys take lots of space, but imaginative packing pays off. A backpack and/or a buggy are well worth any space they take up. Children enjoy choosing and packing the things they want to take. You'll need to set some limits as to types, sizes and number of toys that will be allowed, perhaps by making drawstring bags that limit their choice of things to take. An old brief case of Dad's might also be used.

- Simplify dressing for the whole family by designating specific bags for specific items: 'Susie's clothes', for example, or a night-time suitcase for the whole family. Put children's clothing on top for easy access if you're sharing suitcases.
- Use duffel bags for children's clothes and toys — they'll fit more easily inside the car or boot.
- Save space by taking inflatable toys. When not in use, they

can be deflated and tucked away.

- Pack disposable nappies in the corners of suitcases to save the space a big box will take.
- Let the baby's quilt double as a changing mat if you're taking it with you. Slip it in a pillowcase and tie a ribbon around it to make it easier to carry.
- Pack several large plastic bags. They can be used under sheets for the occasional bedwetter and for dirty washing.
- Take a night light to reassure children who wake up in the night in a strange room.
- Pack a few of the baby's things that will make strange surroundings seem more like home — a cot sheet or blanket that has been in the cot at home for a few days before the trip, one or two toys usually kept in the cot and a plexiglass mirror to put in the new cot so the baby can see himself or herself when waking up.
- Take with you a few electrical socket covers as a travelling child-proofing measure if you'll be staying at a hotel or with people who might not have them.
- Take a small pillow for a child to sit on and to use for sleeps during the journey and at your destination. It's also useful for playing with toys on a lap.
- Put your name and address on pillows, blankets and toys so they can be returned if you leave them behind.
- Take a paper cup for a child who is too old for a bottle, but too small to reach a drinking fountain.
- Keep plasters and pre-moistened wipes in the glove compartment of the car, or in a bag, pocket or in your hand luggage if you're travelling by plane. Remember to put in any medicine or tablets that anyone has to take.
- When you reach your destination consider hiring a playpen or any other equipment you need, but can't take with you.

Comfort in the car

Even if you travel in a large car with plenty of room, you'll want to organize things so that they'll be easy to get at and not cause clutter.

- Make a cover for the front seat of the car with several pockets stitched to the side that will hang over the back for books, games and toys.
- Stuff a pillowcase with bulky cold-weather clothing. You'll have a pillow for sleeping and the clothing will be in one place.

Peace in the car

Parents who travel a lot are used to children's initial excitement and restlessness in the car. The children usually settle down after an hour or so, once seating arrangements and rules have been made.

- Travel at night, or make a very early start, so that the children will sleep in the car, but don't encourage them to sleep too much otherwise they'll be ready to play at night, when you want to sleep.
- Put a small suitcase or box between two children in the back seat to clearly separate 'sides'.
- Place a firm-sided bag filled with small toys and books between two toddlers in car seats. It can be reached easily by the children and holds enough to keep them occupied for quite a distance. Put some of the children's favourite toys and books in the bag well before a trip so they will have more appeal.

- Make seating arrangements changeable. One adult in the back seat for all or half of a trip is usually a good idea.
- Have frequent stops to stretch your legs and play with the children. You'll all need a break. Why not take a skipping rope or inflatable ball to get some exercise and have some fun, too.
- Give the children a five-minute warning before you stop so that they can put on shoes and sweaters or coats.
- Plan — and announce — a treat for the end of the day, so everyone will have something to look forward to: a swim, dinner at a restaurant, a visit to a funfair.
- Take along earplugs for the adults who aren't driving.

Food in the car

If you take an extra set of clothing for each child and a plastic bag for soiled clothes, a spill or an accident won't be a disaster. It's also a good idea to cover the back seat with a sheet or blanket; you can shake out the crumbs when you stop. Keep packaged towelettes handy, or a plastic bottle of water with a little liquid soap added. You can always use the spray from the windscreen wipers, too, if you run out of water.

- Use an insulated bag to keep baby food warm or cold. Tape the baby spoon to one of the jars.
- Make things easy for yourself by taking full jars of meat and fruit, for example, instead of half-jars of three or four different foods.
- Mix instant baby cereal in separate small plastic bags or containers with powdered milk, and add warm water from a thermos when you're ready to feed the baby. Carry frozen baby food cubes in a cool box, with any other food you want to keep cool.
- Take a supply of small paper plates with little slits in the middle. Put the sticks of ice lollies through the slits and there'll be less mess on car seats and fingers.
- Hang a roll for a toddler to munch on a string pinned to his or her clothing or tied around a button or the car seat so it won't fall on the floor.

- Fill several small plastic bags with an assortment of such treats as raisins, nuts and meusli bars, and bring them out when spirits need reviving.
- Take a box of crackers and a tube of cheese spread. The adult who's not driving can decorate the crackers with the cheese in designs, letters or numbers.
- Avoid taking very salty foods in the car — you'll need lots to drink and then you'll have to keep stopping to find toilets.
- Cut sandwiches in different shapes for easy identification: triangles for those with mustard, rectangles for those with mayonnaise, for example.
- Make a mini-ice bucket out of a plastic jug. Put a container of yoghurt or cottage cheese among the ice cubes and the food will stay cold for a few hours.

Eating in restaurants

- Make up your own 'restaurant kit', with children's utensils, snacks, towelettes, a highchair strap or belt, small toys and a plastic clothes peg or nappy pin to fasten a serviette round a child's neck (better still, take a couple of bibs). Restaurant staff will be pleased if you take a newspaper to spread out underneath the highchair. Wrap a couple of thick catalogues or old telephone directories in patterned adhesive paper and take those to use as a booster seat.
- Ask someone to walk around outdoors with an impatient toddler while you're waiting for the food to be served. Or let the child play with ice cubes on the highchair tray, or with paper serviettes or straws.
- Consider wrapping snacks from home for your child in different kinds of food wrap — some, perhaps, even in coloured wrapping paper. It will take lots of time to open all the 'presents'.
- Order a pot of hot water and extra serviettes for cleaning up and, perhaps, to wash a highchair tray that's not quite clean.

Drinks in the car

- Carry a thermos of cold water — it quenches thirst best. Add a little lemon juice for flavour.

- Hang small plastic containers filled with water or juice from the garment hook on each side of the back seat if children are able to handle them.
- Make criss-cross slits in a baby bottle teat; invert and secure it with the cap and cover on a plastic baby bottle filled with your toddler's favourite drink. Remove the cover and insert a straw when he or she wants a drink — no spills.
- Or put the liquids in well-washed plastic lemon juice dispensers. (Remove the inserts with a sharp-pointed object, replace after filling and screw the caps back on.) If you freeze them before you leave, the drinks will stay cool as they melt.
- Satisfy both thirst and hunger with grapes. Oranges serve the same purpose, but they're messier.
- Freeze a half-full plastic container of water. When you're ready to leave, fill the balance of the container with water and you'll have a long-lasting, cold thirst-quencher.
- Don't forget to take one or two nappies to mop up spills — they're very absorbent.

Toys to take with you

- Keep the toy supply in the boot and bring out a few items after every stop, to give variety, returning those in the car to the boot.
- Tie toys to a child's car seat with short strings so that you won't have to keep picking them up.

- Let the children fill school lunch boxes with small toys to play with — but not *so* small that they can get lost in the car.
- Take any small toys your children want in a fabric shoe tidy. Keep it rolled up in the car and it will be ready to hang on a bedroom door when you arrive.
- Wrap up some favourite toys and little surprises using plenty of string and tape. Unwrapping time will give you some peace, but there'll be some litter to clean up in the car.

Activities in the car

Look at your local library for books on games to play and songs to sing in the car. Keep a list of favourite songs and games in the glove compartment so you won't forget them when your children get bored.

- Stick greeting cards, pictures from magazines, even a piece of children's wallpaper to the back of the front seat, so the child in the safety seat will have something interesting to look at.
- While you are in the car make a simple map, so that small children can follow it as well, and mark the places where you are going to stop.
- Put everyone's imagination to the test by 'seeing things' in cloud formations.
- Keep crayons, felt tip pens and colouring books in a biscuit tin. The lid can be used for a work surface. Avoid taking pencils and scissors as their sharp points may be dangerous if you have to stop suddenly.
- Buy magnetized games, or glue pieces of Velcro on board games and their playing pieces, to stop small parts from getting lost. For a dice game, put the dice in a clear plastic jar so that you can just shake them, rather than roll and risk losing them.
- Take along a *big* catalogue for the children to look at.
- Play tapes you've made of favourite stories and songs, or use tapes you've borrowed.

Travel sickness

- Keep a child who's likely to be car sick on a high-carbohydrate, low-fat diet for a few days before a journey and go easy on liquids just before you go.
- Dress your child according to the temperature inside the car — being too warm may increase the chance of nausea.
- If the child is old enough, let him or her sit in the front seat or otherwise high enough in the back so that he or she can look out of the front of the car. The swiftly moving scenery at the side causes nausea.
- Make smooth starts and stops; drive slowly round bends to avoid unnecessary braking.
- Direct the child's attention to things outside the car and a long way off, rather than letting him or her focus on the edge of the road.
- Don't let the child do close work, such as reading or colouring.
- Get the child to wear sunglasses to cut down glare.
- Avoid the smell of strong-flavoured foods or tobacco in the car. Open a window — fresh air often helps.
- When nausea is severe, ask the child to sit in a reclining position with eyes closed and head completely still.
- Take a plastic ice cream container with a lid, or travel sickness bags, in case the child is sick.
- Try hanging a piece of chain (with wire) from the car's rear axle, so that it just touches the ground. This is what lorry drivers who pull loads of flammable liquids use to eliminate electricity, which may cause nausea.
- Consider giving the child a travel sickness pill — but remember that it will only work if it's taken *before* the journey.

Travelling by plane

Babies under two travel free, but you must inform the airline or tour operator that an infant will be travelling with you. If you are going on a scheduled flight, find out from the airline or your travel agent the days of the week and flights which are less crowded. You may then be able to have an extra seat for your baby. (Remember that the trick of travelling by car at night so your children will sleep, doesn't necessarily apply to air travel.) On scheduled flights try to reserve bulkhead seats to give you more leg room and space for your child to stand up, or room for a bassinet if you have a baby. Bassinets are available for you to use behind the bulkheads, but as there are a limited number of bulkhead seats you should make arrangements for a bassinet when you make your booking. Otherwise try to reserve a seat on the aisle to make getting in and out easier. Also remember that there is only limited storage space for hand luggage.

- Attach a luggage tag to your child's clothing, in case you get separated at the airport. Include the child's name and yours, your airline, flight number and destination.

- Try to board the plane with a freshly-nappied baby as generally there's not much room for changing a baby in an aeroplane toilet. (Though some of the larger planes do have drop-down tables in toilets for changing babies.) In any event, it's best to double-nappy the baby and to put on plastic pants. Take a soft fabric shoulder bag for spare nappies, rather than a rigid hand-held one. Put in more nappies than you think you'll need in case of emergencies, though most airlines usually carry spare disposable ones. Travel sickness bags are useful for putting soiled nappies in.

- Don't give your child a sugary snack before boarding; it will make him or her more active. It might be a good idea to take an over-excited child for a walk round the airport to tire him or her out.

- Usually, mothers with babies are allowed to board first to get settled before the other passengers arrive, but ask at the check-in desk to make sure. Also if you want to take your baby's buggy with you, ask at the desk if it is all right to do so.

- If blankets and pillows are available, take them from the overhead rack as you are being seated to make sure of getting them or else ask a stewardess for them.

- Carry a small infant in a baby carrier to avoid his or her slipping out of your arms and to keep your hands free while the baby is asleep. For take-off and landing, though, make sure you are given a seat belt extension for your baby. This slips on to your own seat belt and must be worn at these times.

- Nurse your baby or give a bottle or dummy at take-off and landing, to reduce pressure on ears. Have some boiled sweets for older childen. Blowing up a balloon often helps older children, too. Teach your children to 'swallow' and 'chew' and 'yawn' to open the Eustachian tubes. Play a game of facial movements with your baby. Even the crying some children do when their ears hurt helps equalize pressure imbalance. This is particularly important if a child has a cold or allergies.
- Let a child who is old enough carry his or her own things in a back-pack.
- Take a few new, small toys and books for your children and hand them out one at a time. A pack of cards is a good idea but remember not to take anything that could be dangerous if your child were to throw it.
- Long haul flights usually carry a limited amount of toys, games and puzzles and a stewardess will bring these round to see if your child needs something.
- Don't rush to get off the plane. Well-travelled people say when you have children with you it's best to wait till last to get off.

Food for the flight

There is usually one stewardess allocated to assist mothers and babies and you should always let her know in advance what time you are going to need bottles or food warmed up.

- Always take food with you for your children and your baby. Aeroplane snacks are often biscuits or crunchy things babies shouldn't eat, and if you are delayed you'll have something ready to give to your children. If you do forget to take baby food, the airline will usually have some available, but as it's only a limited supply you shouldn't rely on this.
- If any of your children are on a special diet or are allergic to any particular foods always mention this when you make your booking. The airline will then arrange for special food to be available for those concerned.
- Let children use straws with their drinks — they're fun and

they'll be less likely to spill them. Take a feeding beaker for a child who is too young to use a straw.

- Avoid cola drinks for children. Two or three have as much caffeine as a cup of coffee and they'll make it hard for a child to sit still. They also have a diuretic effect.
- Don't drink hot beverages while your child is on your lap; if they get spilt, your child may be scalded.

Travelling by train

A train ride can be an enjoyable family experience. Children can see the changing countryside and are able to move about much more than in a plane or car.

- If you're reserving seats remember to ask for seats facing each other so you can keep the whole family together.
- Temperatures on trains are not reliable so dress in layers and then clothes can be added or taken off easily.
- Take sandwiches, snacks and drinks with you — restaurant car meals and items from the buffet car may not be suitable for your children. Take some hot water in a thermos flask to warm baby bottles and baby food.

ENJOYING THE OUTDOORS

It's important to remember that children, even responsible pre-school children, must be watched constantly and extra carefully when you're in the woods or near water. Possibilities for fun and learning are there, however. Rainy-day puddles are as exciting as sunsets and wildlife.

Camping with children

Roughing it with small children is not for everyone; if you're not sure you'll like it, choose a campsite with showers, laundry facilities and a shop the first time. You may feel safer if your campsite is not near a road, lake or river. As with any trip, make the most of every moment, even if original plans and destinations have to be changed sometimes.

- Have a practice in your garden. You can try all your equipment and get your children used to living in a tent.

- Include wet weather clothes, boots and jackets when packing, no matter what the weather forecast says. Make washability a priority for camping clothes and, when choosing them, make sure they're suitable for wearing in layers.

- Pack some clothing and equipment in various sized plastic buckets that you can use for washing up, washing clothes and washing yourselves. A large plastic container with a lid makes a good 'mini' washer for small items. Put in some water, add a little powder, put on the lid and shake. Shaking is more efficient than swishing the clothes around in a bucket.

- Use empty plastic food bags for soiled nappies and other wet items.
- Avoid the smell of damp, soiled clothing by packing fabric conditioner sheets in laundry bags.
- Use a small inflatable paddling pool for a child's bath. You can add a quilt or pad and use it as a crib or playpen, too.
- Take a kiddy carrier with you so that you can carry a young child on your back, but build up your 'carrying time' before your trip. And pack a small mirror to use as a 'rear view mirror' while you're hiking.
- Make up a 'nature box', including books on birds, rocks and trees and plenty of plastic bags, jars and boxes to hold collections. Give the children collecting projects: three leaves, five rocks, two cones.
- Pack a first-aid book and a good first-aid kit and include supplies for things like insect bites, sunburn, cuts and bruises. Include tweezers to remove splinters that someone's bound to get.
- Take small empty plastic containers to slip over tent stakes and prevent stubbed toes.
- Take food and drink in the car at all times, even if you plan to buy most of it at your campsite, so that you're prepared for anything.
- Think about taking your own drinking water with you, if you don't trust the water at the campsite. You *don't* want the children to get diarrhoea!

On the beach

- Remember that children burn much more easily than adults. Put hats on small children, and use a good sun screen cream on their skin.
- Use a big sheet for children to sit on instead of a blanket or towel. It's cooler, sand will shake off easily, and it will fold neatly and compactly for storage.

- Put beach gear, if there's a lot of it, into a plastic sledge to pull across the sand.
- Or carry beach toys in a plastic laundry basket or mesh bag that you can dunk in the water for a quick rinse and drain at the end of the day.
- Mark your beach toys. Yours will probably look like everyone else's.
- Put large jar lids under the legs of a playpen, if you take it on the beach, to stop them sinking into the sand. (This works well in your garden at home, too.)
- Turn a playpen upside down over a blanket or sheet to keep the hot sun off a child and the child off the hot sand. Or put up a large umbrella over a blanket.

- Remove nappies when giving a baby a swim. They absorb too much water and become very heavy so that the baby loses natural buoyancy.
- Fill a child's bucket with water when leaving the beach and get the children to dip their feet in it before getting into the car.
- Or dust baby powder over children's sandy, dry arms and legs. Brush off the powder and sand together.

Chapter Eight

Child's Play

Child's play is learning, and many who have studied child development say that the more imaginative the play, the more a child may learn. Most parents have seen a child become more fascinated with the box a toy comes in than with the toy itself. This is not to say, 'Don't buy toys', but to suggest that the fun and learning of play can depend upon what's at hand as well.

SEASONAL FUN

A climate like that of a tropical island would seem like a dream come true to parents of active children — warm weather all year round ... no gloves, hats, scarves or jackets. Most children, though, like the break between summer and winter activities.

Warm-weather specials

- Fill a flour shaker with cornflour and let the children sprinkle everything in sight outdoors. The first shower will clean things up.
- Let the children draw on your garden path with coloured chalk.
- Make a sandpit from an old plastic paddling pool or a fish pond liner. Sink it into the ground and fill it with coarse sand, not the fine variety.

- Hang blankets over the clothes-line to make a tent. Or put up a real tent for your children to sleep in at night or even for a daytime nap.
- Attach a special baby swing to the older children's swing so that they can all swing together.
- Put an old rubber doormat or a piece of carpeting under the swing to protect shoes and to keep some of the dirt outdoors.
- Let your child help you with garden chores, or give him or her a small plot to look after. Choose quick-growing things such as lettuce, beans, radishes or marigolds.

Water play

- Put the baby bath, filled with water, under the baby's walker for kicking fun.
- Make a water pistol from an empty plastic washing-up liquid bottle or a roast baster.
- Put a plastic paddling pool at the bottom of the slide on a hot day and let the children slide down into the water.
- Fill balloons three-quarters full of water, close them with twist ties so they can be used again, and throw them around the garden.
- Let them paint the house with water and a big brush, or add food colouring to the water and let them paint the paths.
- Give a child a bowl of water, add washing-up liquid and let him or her whip up suds with a beater. Then give the child a plastic straw to blow bubbles with.
- Make a very small hole in the bottom of a tin, attach it to your child's tricycle and fill it with coloured water. The child's ride lasts until the 'petrol' has run out.
- If you can stand the mess, a mudhole in the corner of your garden can surpass even a sandpit for children's enjoyment.
- Let the children wash the car. It may not be uniformly clean, but they'll have fun. Or let them wash tricycles, bikes or toys.

Snowy-day specials

- Use an old plastic baby bath for a sledge. (Punch a hole in the rim and attach a rope.) It won't go too fast, and the sides will stop a small child falling out.
- Let a toddler use a dustpan for a snow shovel — right size, right height.
- Teach the children to play a game of chase in the snow. Draw a big circle by shuffling through the snow and bisect it two ways, at right angles. The players can run only on the lines.
- Or show them how to make angels in the snow by lying down spread-eagled, moving arms up and down and legs together and apart.

- Fill a plastic squeezy or spray bottle with water to which you have added food colouring, so children can draw in the snow or 'paint' a snowman.
- Put special marks on a large outdoor thermometer so children know when they have to wear jackets, boots and other thick clothing. (And also mark summer temperatures — when it's warm enough for picnics and water play.)
- Rub petroleum jelly into children's cheeks to protect them in cold or windy weather.
- Put inexpensive rubber gloves on over children's ordinary gloves to keep their hands dry.

Too bad to go out

- Let the children play with snow in the kitchen sink, or with lots of snow in the bath. Cover them up with raincoats worn backwards or outdoor play clothes. (This activity is best at floor-washing time as things might get messy.)

- Help children with a little experiment: bring a bowl of snow inside and show them how little water it makes when it melts.
- Let the children relax in the bath for a while before nap-time or bedtime to get warm and sleepy.

INDOORS AND OUT

You can buy lots of expensive toys and equipment that are educational and fun for children to play with and you can take your children to places where they'll learn a lot and enjoy themselves. But you can also supply inexpensive things for them to play with which will provide hours of fun.

Playhouses, castles, etc

- Drape an old sheet over a folding table to make a playhouse that can be put up and taken down in minutes. Cut or draw windows and doors and let the children decorate the sheet by drawing flowers and bricks with felt-tip pens.
- Use a very large cardboard box for a playhouse. Cut out doors and windows and let the children draw curtains, rugs and pictures inside and shrubbery, door lights and a doorbell outside. Remember that large cartons also make castles, tunnels, trains, boats — the only limit is the imagination.
- Cover the top of an old wooden playpen with a sheet of plywood and remove three or four rails from one side: an instant playhouse.
- Hang bedspreads, sheets or blankets over chairs (hold them in place with pegs) for a secret hide-out.
- Make train or aeroplane seats for several children with chairs and stools from all over the house.
- Spread magazines or cushions around the floor to make 'rooms' and to use as stepping stones. Or use carpet squares for 'magic carpets'.
- Put an old mattress on the floor for tumbling and jumping on to save wear and tear on chairs, couches and beds.

- Make a doll's house by fixing together four boxes of the same size, two up and two down. Cut out windows and doors. Give the children scraps of material, wallpaper or carpeting and let them decorate it.

Games

- Make a 'busy box' for a toddler, with things to spin, a bell to ring, a lock and key, a chain to rattle, knobs and balls — all attached to a heavy cardboard box.
- Make an indoor sandtray out of any sturdy box or shallow tray and fill it with used coffee grounds (speed-up the drying process in the oven). It's ideal for roads for little cars.
- Give an old shower curtain new life and map out on it, with a heavy felt-tip pen, a village full of roads and railway lines. The children can spread it out and play with their cars, lorries and trains.
- Give a toddler an empty paper towel tube and a round balloon for a safe, easy-to-use bat and ball game. All kinds of tubes also make good tunnels for little cars.
- Make a 'wicket' for plastic bat-and-ball play by stacking two fizzy drink cans on top of each other. Children have as much fun knocking over the cans as they do hitting the ball.
- Paint small, empty cans or plastic bottles and let the children use them for skittles, with a small rubber ball.
- Get out a box of old clothes and let the children play at dressing-up. Use old cot blankets for capes, skirts and veils.

- Give children scraps of wrapping paper, sticky tape and pieces of ribbon to have a 'birthday party', wrapping and tying their own toys for presents.
- Play dice games with little children, who find dice easier to handle than cards. You can make dice from erasers cut in half and decorated with the usual dots or your own symbols.
- Let children who can't manage cards hold them with pegs.

Playing Games with Children: Win or Lose?
Lose without 'cheating' by using a handicap system that you devise. In draughts, for example, change sides every three moves. Or make a rule that no player can be more than one captured piece ahead.

Puzzles

- Glue small unpainted furniture knobs from a DIY shop onto puzzle pieces to make them easier for little children to handle. The knobs can be painted to match the pieces.
- Make puzzles by pasting large, clear pictures on heavy cardboard and covering them with clear adhesive paper. Cut with a sharp knife or small saw into as many as 25 pieces, even for a pre-school child, in distinctly different shapes — stars, triangles, arrows, circles, squares.
- Stop puzzles getting hopelessly jumbled up by marking the backs of all pieces of one puzzle with one colour, another puzzle with a different colour, and so on. They will be easier to sort by the colour on the back than by the design on the front.

Things to 'unmake' and 'undo'

- Remember that any appliance or gadget on its way to the dustbin offers fascinating possibilities for unscrewing, opening and taking apart, even breaking.
- Look for broken clocks, record players or cameras at jumble sales.
- Let the children help with any dismantling project in the house or garden — a wall being taken down, a garden dug, a path being broken up.

Cleaning and repairing toys

- Save work by buying machine-washable stuffed toys and dishwasher-safe plastic toys.
- Clean and deodorize toys by wiping them with a moist cloth dipped in baking soda.
- Shake stuffed toys in a bag with a generous amount of cornflour or baking powder. Brush it out afterwards and the dirt will come away with it.
- Or use carpet shampoo and a brush to clean stuffed toys.
- Clean cloth dolls by making a paste of soap flakes and water, applying it with a toothbrush, and wiping off with a damp cloth.
- Paint clear nail polish over the ceramic face of a doll to freshen it. And paint paper dolls with nail polish to stop them tearing.
- Apply two or three coats of nail polish to pinholes in inflatable toys.
- Soak plastic toys that have got out of shape in hot water, then work them back into shape.
- Tape strips of masking tape over the corners of boxes of games and puzzles *before* they break. And preserve board games, puzzles and even book covers with generous coats of clear varnish, clear lacquer or clear adhesive paper. All will make the items easy to clean.
- Cut circles from a wooden broom handle; sand and paint them to replace lost draughts.

ARTS AND CRAFTS

Don't ask a child who's being creative, 'What is it?', say those who work with children in arts and crafts. Such a question puts a child on the spot. Instead, talk about colours, thickness or thinness of paint, interesting shapes. Save trouble when children are doing messy work by getting them to wear an adult's old shirt with the sleeves shortened. You can save more trouble if you have a tiled floor, or put down plastic carpet protector or a piece of vinyl floor covering in the children's 'creative corner'. Covering the work table also makes cleaning-up easy.

Painting

Investigate free or inexpensive sources of interesting kinds of paper: rolls of discontinued black-and-white wallpaper for colouring; shelf paper; ends of rolls of newsprint from your local newspaper; brown paper bags. Save nappy boxes with white insides and cut them up for painting on. Or make a writing or colouring board by covering a piece of cardboard with clear adhesive paper. Erase with a dampened tissue or paper towel.

- Make finger paint for children with water or paste and food colouring.
- Or mix shaving cream with food colouring and let your child paint on shiny paper, to have some gooey fun.
- Or let your child finger-paint with cooking oil on baking trays.
- Buy powdered water colours and mix only the amount needed, in small jars or plastic egg cartons.
- Mix powdered paint with flour and water instead of water to get a better consistency for beginners.
- Or make instant paint by adding a few drops of food colouring to a little dissolved starch powder in a small container.
- Use an ashtray with cigarette rests and double-suction

pads underneath as a water dish — it provides somewhere to put a brush and won't tip over.

- Insert water or paint containers into holes you've cut in a big synthetic sponge to prevent them being spilt and to soak up any excess liquid.
- Mix a little washing powder with finger paints or poster paints to make cleaning up easy.
- Save trips to the sink for cleaning hands by putting some paper towels and a spray bottle filled with water on the table.

Brushes

- Let beginners paint with pastry brushes, which pick up a lot of paint. Or let them use cotton wool buds or pipe cleaners with ends twisted into loops for painting that doesn't require fine line work.
- Get toddlers' brushes from a DIY shop. Brushes used for painting window frames are wide enough and have short handles.
- Fill a cleaned-out roll-on deodorant bottle with paint and let the children roll paint on.

Recycling wax crayons

- Sharpen crayons by dipping them in hot water and rolling them to a point between your thumb and forefinger.
- Make 'double colour' crayons by removing the paper from two of the same length, melting one side of each over a candle flame and letting them solidify together. Or tie three or four different colour crayons together with a rubber band.
- Melt old crayons of the same colour (with paper removed) in empty cans placed in hot water over a medium heat on the cooker. Pour the wax into the cups of an old bun tin, cool and turn out — fun crayons for young children.

Glue

- Use liquid starch as glue for children. It works well on tissue paper collages, cut-outs, overlays or assembly work and it dries overnight.

- Use up old clear nail polish as glue; the little brush is a good size for a child. Refill the empty bottle with glue, too.
- Put glue in one section of a plastic egg carton and the small items to be glued — macaroni, beans, rice, whatever — in other sections.
- Keep paste fresh and smooth by adding a few drops of water to it before closing the jar.
- Lubricate the cap grooves of glue and paste containers with petroleum jelly to make them easy to open and close.

Storing materials

- Put up a towel rail to use as a dispenser for a big roll of shelf paper for children's drawing and painting activities. Hang a pair of blunt-ended scissors nearby so that children can help themselves.
- Use a kitchen cutlery tray to store art supplies and keep them separated.
- Poke holes in a block of polystyrene with a felt tip pen and stand all felt tip pens up in the block to keep them together and to make it easier to choose colours.
- Keep crayons in clean yogurt or cottage cheese pots when the boxes are broken.
- Store felt-tipped pens in sealed jars to stop them drying out.

Preserving drawings

- Preserve a wax crayon drawing by putting it face-up on the ironing board (with brown paper underneath to protect the pad) and laying over it a piece of cotton sheeting. Iron the fabric firmly at a low to medium setting until the drawing has been transferred to the cloth, and let it cool before moving it.
- Spray drawings with hair spray to preserve the paper and to stop the colours rubbing off.
- Or soak drawings in a solution which, it has been claimed, will give them 'an estimated life of 200 years'. Dissolve a milk of magnesia tablet in a quart of soda water and leave it

overnight. Soak the paper in the solution for an hour, pat it dry and don't move it until it's completely dry.

Your 'artist' on display

Save artwork *you* like; let the children keep the things *they* like; and encourage throwing away pieces no one particularly likes. You'll cut down on the number to be kept and you'll be helping your childen be more critical of their own work. Your praise will be credible, too.

- Let the children write notes to their grandparents on the backs of drawings, saving paper as well as getting the artwork out into the world where it will be appreciated.
- Let them make gift wrapping paper by decorating white shelf paper with crayons or paints.
- Take pictures of your child standing by a display of his or her work stuck on the refrigerator with magnets or displayed somewhere else. Later you can all look back and see the fine drawings that were done.
- Use a big piece of cardbord as a board to hang paintings on when the refrigerator door is full.
- Attach drawings to painted surfaces with dabs of toothpaste on the four corners.
- Show your appreciation of a child's artwork by hanging a painting in the living room in a frame with an easily removable back. Change the painting frequently.
- Make placemats from drawings or paintings by sealing them between two layers of clear adhesive paper. Or insert them in plastic folders for changeable placemats.
- Use a clear plastic tablecloth and display drawings under it. Or, if you have a glass table, stick the drawings, face-up, to the underside of the glass.
- Let children stick drawings on baby milk tins, coffee tins or other tins with plastic lids. They make good gift containers and are reusable as containers for art supplies and other small objects.
- Punch holes in drawings and keep them in a loose-leaf folder. Or let children keep the drawings they want by clipping them together with giant, coloured plastic clips.

GETTING READY FOR SCHOOL

The decision to send a child to nursery school is an individual one, determined by personal preference, family finances, availability of playmates and other factors. Those who like the idea of nursery school say it helps prepare children for infant school and helps them learn to relate to adults other than their parents and adjust to the company of other children. Those who don't like the idea feel that with a little effort they can provide appropriate learning experiences at home and, often, that they just aren't ready to let their children go.

Organizing for school

- Set the school-night bedtime before school starts and stick to it. Get up early yourself and get on with things that you would be doing on a normal school day.
- Get school clothes together and involve the child as much as possible in choosing new ones.
- Start the routine of selecting and laying out the next day's clothes the night before, including shoes and socks. Get your child into the habit of dressing completely before breakfast.
- Walk to school or the bus stop with your child several times. Discuss the best way to get there and talk about any dangers on the way, such as busy road junctions.

Learning Left from Right
A child can form the letter L by holding up the left hand, fingers together and thumb stuck out straight . . . and learn two things at once. Or, if the child is right-handed, he or she 'writes with the right'.

Off-to-school routines

It's usually helpful for a child to visit the nursery or infant school and meet the teacher before the first day, if possible. Many schools have an open day to which both parents and pupils are invited — if your school does, try not to miss it.

- Set a timer so your child knows when it's time to gather belongings and get ready to leave for school.
- Attach name tags to any clothes that the child will be taking

off at school — sweaters, jackets etc.

- Give your child an empty paper towel tube for carrying important papers to and from school. In rainy weather, the tube can be slipped into a plastic bag to keep it dry.
- Or get the child a school bag or small back-pack — either is very grown-up. (And a back-pack won't wear out from being dragged on the ground, as a bag will.)
- Keep old nappy pins handy to pin notes to the teacher on the child's clothing.
- Let Dad drop your child at school the first few days, if he's the one who usually goes off to work. The child will be used to saying goodbye to him and it won't be so hard.
- Make sure your child understands that no one but a parent (or other designated person) can collect him or her from school without written permission.
- Don't forget to ask each day about school activities. Listen very carefully to the answers in order to head off any problems. (Some children will tell you more than others; don't give your child the 'third degree'!) You may find that the best time to ask about the day's events is at night when you are tucking your child into bed.
- Draw a big map including the home-to-school route and put in local landmarks. Let your child play on it with small cars or dolls.
- Talk about what school will be like a lot, but be careful not to promise anything you're not sure will happen. Listen carefully to your child to find out if he or she is frightened or worried about anything. Something that might seem silly to you is very real to your child, so try putting yourself in the child's place.
- Ask your child into recite his or her full name, address and phone number frequently.
- Try role-playing, and let the child play both pupil and teacher.
- Give your child two gifts to help him or her with the new routine: an alarm clock — and start setting it for bedtime and waking-up time — and a calendar on which he or she can mark and cross off special days, weekends and holidays.

Chapter Nine

Special Situations

The topics of the first eight chapters of this book apply to parents and children in general. The sections in this chapter apply to those whose situations are 'a little bit different', in one way or another. Here are the tips of parents who have been in these special situations and who have learned the best ways — for them, at least — of dealing with certain circumstances.

CAESAREAN DELIVERIES

If you know you are going to have a caesarean section, you can make some decisions before you go into hospital. If you want the father to be present, find out if this will be possible. Ask for minimal local anaesthetic, if that's what you want. Plan to nurse the baby immediately after the anaesthetic has worn off, if you are going to breastfeed. In most hospitals the baby will be in a cot by your bed, so you will be able to establish your own feeding routine. The National Childbirth Trust produces an informative leaflet on caesarean birth. It costs 30p plus 30p for postage and packing and is available from them at Alexandra House, Oldham Terrace, Acton, London W3 6NH.

When you get home

- Stay in bed as much as you can. Keep the baby in a crib or cot by your bed, with a good supply of nappies and baby clothes handy.

- Get a nightdress robe that buttons all the way down the front. You'll find getting into and out of it easier than stepping in and out of one that opens only part of the way down.
- Wear a protective panty girdle to keep loose clothing from rubbing on your tender wound.
- Use a hair dryer to dry your wound thoroughly after a bath to prevent rubbing the tender area with a towel.
- Put a pillow on your lap when nursing, both to support the baby and to protect your wound.
- Try making a playpen of your bed, if you have a toddler to look after, too. Keep toys and books within reach.

Caring for tender abdominal muscles

- Use your foot as a lever to lift a toddler up to you when you are in a chair or in bed, rather than bending down to pick him or her up from the floor.
- Use a high changing table, not a bed, to avoid bending down when you dress the baby.
- Try to avoid holding the baby in one arm while you work around the house until your muscles are stronger. Try using a wind-up baby swing if the baby is making a fuss and wants attention.

- Don't vacuum for a couple of months — the particular movements involved are hardest on abdominal muscles. It's an ideal job for a father or another family member to take over.

TWINS

'Help!' is the first cry of parents of multiple births. And help of every kind is what's needed, right from day one. Your friends, neighbours or relatives may offer, and don't be too proud to accept. Remember that it's very important to make time for yourself, even to the point of going away for a weekend if that's the only way you can do it.

Equipment

- Get only about one-and-a-half times the number of everyday items for twins that you'd have for a single baby — nappies, sleeping suits, vests, bibs, sheets and plastic pants — especially in the very small sizes that are quickly outgrown.
- Beg, borrow or buy two of some basic pieces of equipment, such as car safety seats, highchairs (folding ones are good for travelling and save space at home) and playpens. You'll be able to get by with one cot for a few months by putting one baby at each end. (But you may find that they move around in order to be next to each other, seeking their prenatal environment.)
- Use wind-up baby swings or baby bouncers as a substitute for cuddling when you're busy, or to quieten irritable or overtired babies.
- Consider turning the twins' room into a more comfortable and convenient play area and doing without playpens altogether. Put a safety gate on the door frame to keep the toddlers in and you'll be able to keep an eye on them, too. Careful child-proofing!
- See if a twin buggy would be useful for you. There are basically two types available — a swivel wheel type which gives easier manoeuvrability and a fixed wheel type. Before buying one, check to find out which is going to suit you best. If you already have a single buggy, it is possible to buy a

special clip to join on another buggy. Later, you could push one twin in a buggy and carry the other in a kiddy carrier on your back.

Telling one from the other

- Put nail polish on a toenail of one twin to help you tell identical twins apart.
- Colour code nappy pins, or tie different coloured ankle ribbons on the twins.
- Or dress them in different coloured clothes — one always in red, the other in blue. (They'll probably object to wearing the same colour all the time when they're older, but you'll be able to tell then apart by then.)
- Put a bracelet on one. Or cut a bit of one's hair.
- Keep the shoes of toddler twins separate by lacing one pair over, the other under, in the two bottom holes. Or tie a knot in the centre of one twin's shoelaces.

Feeding two

- Note which breast you used for the last feed of each twin, if you're nursing, and switch sides for each feed to encourage the babies' eye muscle control.
- Use small bottles for feeding when the babies are little. Twins are usually smaller than other babies and take less at each feed.
- Avoid filling up your refrigerator with bottles by making up formula as you need it, as you would instant coffee. Or make a big batch and store it in a large sterilized bottle. If you make it double strength, you can add hot boiled water to bring it to room temperature.
- Bottle-feed two hungry babies at once in bouncing cradles on the floor — but make sure you're comfortable before you start.
- Give yourself a little time to prepare a meal by putting twins about four months old in highchairs with blanket rolls on both sides to brace them and give them something to play with.
- Save time and energy by feeding both twins with the same

spoon from the same bowl (or straight from the jar) when they're ready for solids. They're bound to share most germs, anyway.

- Save time by feeding the morning cereal in the twins' bottles, with teats cut larger. You can carry on doing this even when you're spoon feeding other meals.
- Feed the babies their lunch and dinner before the rest of the family until they can handle eating alone well. You deserve and need an undisturbed meal at least once a day.

Daily routines

When the twins are tiny you'll find it easier to keep the same routine for both of them, even if it means waking one for a feed. Put them down for sleeps at the same time from the beginning in order to establish a routine which gives you a little time for yourself.

- Don't try to bath two tiny babies at once; it's better to have one screaming in the cot than two screaming in the bath.
- Keep charts at the ends of the babies' cots to record feeds, stools and baths to save confusion and mix-ups.
- Try to have a sitter with you occasionally to help. When you leave your twins with a sitter, you'll probably prefer a mature, experienced person; consider having two teenage sitters to share the duties if an older person isn't available.
- Take comfort when both babies scream at the same time — it almost always means that it's just 'crying time' and that there's nothing really wrong with either.
- Once the babies can crawl or walk, sit down on the floor and let them come to you for cuddling without lifting them up and risking hurting your back.
- Don't be surprised if your twins are a bit slow in talking (or in any other aspect of development). If they were premature, you may want to think of them in terms of their gestational (expected birth) age rather than their chronological age. And remember that they have each other; they may not *need* to talk.
- Train yourself never to shout at your twins, or you'll be shouting twice as much as other mothers. And from the beginning resign yourself to the fact that most things take

twice as long to do. You don't want to bring up children who are always being rushed.

- Speak clearly and distinctly to *each* twin, and wait for *each* to answer, to help avoid the development of a special language that only they will speak and understand and to be sure that one doesn't start to answer for both.
- Child-proof your home extra carefully. What one pair of eyes doesn't see, the other will.

Treating twins 'like other children'

- Avoid any implications, right from the start, that your twins are a 'matched set'. Use their names, instead of calling them 'the twins', encourage separation sometimes and don't *always* dress them alike. Encourage other-than-twin nicknames as they grow older.
- Be careful not to make remarks in front of your twins, even when they're tiny, about their being 'double trouble' and 'twice the work', and don't allow others to do so.
- Try to treat twins even-handedly and make sure you know which one is 'dominant'. The twin who seems to be the 'passive' one may effectively manipulate the other and get his or her own way most of the time.

- Be sure to take individual pictures of the twins. They will probably need baby pictures for school one day, and a picture of oneself alone helps build self-confidence.
- Have two birthday cakes, especially as the twins get older.
- Remember that identical twins often need more togetherness than fraternal twins, but as they grow, try to get them interested in different activities and separate them sometimes.

Twins and Multiple Births Association

'Tamba', an organisation founded to help and advise parents of twins and multiple offspring born at one birth may be contacted at:

Pooh Corner,
54 Broad Lane,
Hampton,
Middlesex TW12 3BG
Telephone: 01-941 0641

ADOPTED CHILDREN

Parenthood is the ongoing process and responsibility of caring for a child. Whether the child is biologically yours or adopted, your job as a parent is the same. While adoption doesn't allow you the nine months of anticipation usually allotted by a pregnancy, remember that those nine months don't allow a natural parent to be fully prepared for the unanticipated demands of parenthood, either.

From the beginning

- For help and advice about adoption, contact your local Social Services department. They can either arrange an adoption for you or give you the names of recognized adoption agencies.
- If you have never given birth, you might like to make arrangements to visit the ante-natal clinic at your local hospital to find out about the ante-natal care so you will be completely comfortable with the idea of birth.
- Ask those with whom you work at the Social Services or

agency to suggest books about adoption for both adults and children.

- Tell your child from the beginning that he or she came into the family by adoption, but talk more about your family relationships than about the adoption procedure.
- Avoid using clichés that make things seem unnaturally rosy and set your child apart as special. 'We chose you from all the others' is one such cliché.
- Don't make a practice of celebrating the day your child joined your family — more than one 'birthday' makes a child different from others and may embarrass him or her.
- If possible get as much information about your child's natural parents as you can and tell the child realistic details about their looks and sizes, hobbies, talents and interests.
- Keep the child informed about the progress of the adoption. If the child is old enough, he or she must be consulted and agree with the adoption arrangement.
- Help another child to accept the new child into the family by talking about the arrangement as much as possible, and using terms such as 'your brother (or sister)' and 'our family' consistently.
- Include your family and close friends in the celebration of adoption as you would at a wedding or christening.

Adopting a child from a foreign country

Adopting children from another country is very complicated legally and quite difficult to achieve, and, in Britain, no agencies will arrange adoptions of children from overseas. Under immigration rules, a child cannot come to Britain for adoption without entry clearance. A representative should apply to the nearest British Government official where the child is living for the child to come to the United Kingdom. If entry clearance is authorised, the child will be admitted initially for a short period, but this can be extended if the adoption hearing is not held within that period. The adoption order for a child from overseas must be granted by a British court. For tactical advice about adopting a child from another country, contact either the United Kingdom Immigrants Advisory Service, 2nd Floor, County House, 190 Great Dover Street, London SE1 4YB. Telephone: 01-357 6917 or the Joint Council for the Welfare of Immigrants, 115 Old St., London EC1. Telephone: 01-251 5674. If you are successful in adopting a child from overseas remember that while the child will become a member of your family, he or she can never be fully assimilated – it's cruel and unrealistic to let such a child think he or she is 'just like you'. The more thoroughly you are able to familiarize yourself with such things as the other country's religion and holidays, social and family relationships, the better you will be equipped to help your child retain his or her cultural identity and racial pride. As marriage may bring new cultural dimensions to a family, so may the adoption of a child from abroad.

- Don't allow yourself to be discouraged if your child seems less than perfectly healthy when he or she arrives. Most illnesses are treatable and reversible, and seeing your child back to full health can deepen your bonds with each other.
- And don't worry if he or she seems behind in development. Undernourishment and the understimulation of life in an orphanage may be responsible, and both can be corrected.
- Put off a visit to a doctor for at least 24 hours after your child's arrival — the testing and handling necessary in a check-up are liable to be frightening. And delay dental care, if at all possible, until your child is adjusted to your family (and the language, if he or she is talking).
- Try to maintain a loose, relaxed routine for a time; children from some cultures live unstructured, flexible lives, especially with regard to eating and sleeping.
- Respect your child's habit of sleeping with an adult or another child when he or she first arrives, if that is what he or she has been used to and you can manage it.
- Expect some behavioural changes in toddlers and pre-school-children — regression in toilet training, increased irritability, sleep problems, aggressive behaviour. They're all natural reactions to a changed lifestyle.
- Let your child keep any personal items he or she may have brought along, even if they don't meet your standards of cleanliness or you don't think they are appropriate.
- If your child shows signs of being unable to digest milk, speak to your doctor about it. Children from many cultures have difficulty digesting milk and suffer from cramp and

diarrhoea if they are given it.

- Let your child mix with other children from his or her own country and culture, if possible, especially if he or she is old enough to talk.

SINGLE PARENTS

A dependable support system is essential for a single parent. It's not a sign of weakness to seek support; in reality, it's a sign of strength to be able to admit that you can't do everything, be everything, all alone. Your support may come from family, friends or one of the established support groups listed on page 170.

Try to look on the bright side of single parenting. Some of the things that could be considered disadvantages can be thought of as advantages. For example, you have to make all the decisions, but you can make the ones you *want* and *think are right*. And your child may well turn out to be more responsible, helpful and independent than some of those with two parents.

If you're a divorced single parent, don't ask your child to be a messenger between parents, however much you may be tempted to do so, and don't pump the child for details of the other person's life.

Divorced parents, with custody

Even though you and your spouse may not be able to get on, remember that your children need two parents. Parents should

strive for basic agreement on general matters of child rearing so they don't undermine each other's efforts.

- Expect some behavioural changes in toddlers and pre-school children — regression in toilet training, increased irritability, fear, sleep problems, aggressive behaviour. They're all natural reactions to a changed life.
- But remember that your child's problems will more often than not be normal development phases, due neither to the divorce nor to the single parent situation.
- Make sure your child understands that he or she is not responsible in any way for the divorce. You cannot repeat this too often!
- Give your child more of your time, if it seems necessary, but not *all* your time. You need your own hobbies and friends.
- Be open with your child about any changes in your financial situation.
- Eat out as often as your budget allows. You need the break and your children do, too.
- Don't try to carry on the same holiday routines. Bring in new people, start new traditions. Try new holiday locations, if you can.

Visiting your child

- Try to arrange visits in different places — the custodial home, where your child can play host; restaurants; your own home; places where you can go together.
- Don't rule out others being present during visits, but don't *always* include another person; you and your child need time alone together.
- Visit your child as often as has been agreed. Meeting-up for lunch regularly is one way.
- Give full, honest explanations to your child if you have to cancel or postpone a visit.
- Try to do some things with your child by phone, if you can't visit as often as has been arranged. You might arrange to watch a TV programme 'together' and discuss it by phone, to listen to a radio programme or to read together over the phone.

Support Groups for Single Parents
The following groups have been set up to provide moral and emotional support, friendship, advice and help for single parents.

Gingerbread
35 Wellington Street, London WC2E 7BN
Telephone: 01-240 0953

One Parent Families
255 Kentish Town Road, London NW5 2LX
Telephone: 01-267 1361

Singlehanded Ltd
Thorne House,
Hankham Place,
Stone Cross,
Pevensey,
East Sussex BN24 5ER
Telephone: Eastbourne (0323) 767507

Cruse (An organisation which helps widows, widowers and their children)
Cruse House,
126 Sheen Road,
Richmond,
Surrey TW9 1UR
Telephone: 01-940 4818

STEP-PARENTING

The 'move-in' parent is usually the one who must be most willing and able to adjust to established routines and patterns. He or she must try to know all the rules, considerations and conditions before taking on the new role — and be prepared for them all to change.

The parent who leaves his or her own children and subsequently assumes care and responsibility for stepchildren often feels very guilty and may unconsciously withhold affection from the stepchildren.

Those who have gone through the step-parenting experience say real adjustment may take several years, but that it's all well worth the effort.

First meetings

- Make the first meeting with prospective stepchildren a casual, not a formal one which requires elaborate preparation.

- Meet on neutral territory — a restaurant or park, perhaps — and have a specific plan of what you are going to do. Making conversation may be difficult, but doing something you all enjoy, probably won't.
- Don't take presents to a first meeting (unless it's a birthday party). It might look as if you are trying to offer bribes.

Living as a new family

- Don't surprise your children with a new marriage and/or a new house. Let them know what's happening. Avoid over excitement and admit that there will be problems and that you'll all work to try and overcome them.
- Start your new family in a new house or flat, if it's *at all* possible (and especially if more than one set of children is involved), in order to cut down on territorial feelings.
- Don't expect instant love to develop between stepchildren and step-parents, or between stepbrothers and stepsisters, just as you wouldn't expect it with a new baby. Don't rush things and let affection develop over a period of time.
- Let all the children participate in deciding what the step-

parent will be called. Some want to use Mummy/Daddy straightaway to give them a secure family feeling; others don't. First names may work best, or nicknames could be invented.

- Refer to your stepchild as 'our son' or 'my daughter' when the occasion arises, rather than as your stepchild. This is hard to do at first, but it's fundamental for a good relationship.
- Discuss adopting the stepchild, if it's being considered, with the child. Taking the new family's name may offer security to some children, but others may wish to retain their original names. Grandparents may also have wishes you want to consider.
- Let the natural parent do as much of the disciplining of a child as possible at first — share it gradually. This is a particularly tricky challenge for a stepmother, who may spend more time with a child than the father does.
- Talk about rules, limitations and unfamiliar parenting situations with your spouse. Discuss arrangements in private so children won't feel a sense of insecurity and uncertainty.

The visiting child

- Make sure the visiting child (and any who live there) understands that it's his or her home, too.
- Let the child have a room of his or her own, if possible, or at least a cupboard, shelf or drawer for his or her possessions, which will not be disturbed between visits.
- Give the child a proper place at the table, so he or she won't feel like an intruder.
- Let the visiting child have a few days to settle in on a long visit before starting a round of activities.
- Include the child in household chores and projects as well as in excursions and play, to help him or her feel a part of family life and to make the other children accept the visitor as one of the family.
- Make sure the visiting child and his or her natural parent have some time alone together. This may occasionally

mean a step-parent going out for a few hours or even away for a couple of days.

- Save the *best* — be it a gift or an activity — for last, so a visit ends on a high note.
- *Sometimes* before a child leaves plan some nice things to do on his or her next visit, so there will be something to look forward to. Making a point of *always* doing this, though, is unnatural and may make the children who live with you all the time feel jealous.

The National Stepfamily Association

'Stepfamily' is an association set up to offer practical help, support, information and advice to all members of stepfamilies.

The National Stepfamily Association
162 Tenison Road,
Cambridge CB1 2DP
Telephone: (0223) 460312

LEFT-HANDERS

In Grandma's day it wasn't unusual to hear that the right hand was the 'angel's hand' and the left the 'devil's hand'. Few people today are so thoughtless, but right-handed parents might look closely at such tools as ladles, butter knives and tin openers — and even certain toys — before they label left-handed children awkward. A left-handed child may be encouraged to try doing some things, such as cutting with the right hand to save trouble for himself or herself later, but *don't force it*!

- Don't make such a big thing of a child being left-handed that he or she feels handicapped. Making a point of always seating the child at the end of the table, for example, draws unnecessary attention to him or her and starts a habit that can't always be followed.
- Provide left-handed scissors from the start, because right-handed ones simply don't work very well for left handers. And make sure that your child's school provides them, or give your child a pair to take.

- Suggest that the child turn right-handed scissors upside down, if he or she has to use them sometimes.
- Tilt paper to the right instead of the left when your left-handed child begins to draw and write, to avoid awkward and often inconvenient 'hooked hand' writing later.
- Teach your left-hander to cross the left-hand lace over the right in order to get a straight bow.
- Try getting a left-handed child to follow your movements in the reflection of a mirror when he or she needs to imitate something you are doing to learn a new skill.
- Buy some special left-handed equipment to make your child's life easier and to add a little fun — a mug with the child's name on the front and the handle on the left, a T-shirt with a slogan across it.

Equipment for the left-handed
Anything Left Handed Ltd, 65 Beak Street, London W1R 3LF, Telephone 01-437 3910, *offer a range of approximately 150 items specifically designed for left-handers – from scissors and pens to instruction booklets on knitting and crochet – and all are available by mail order. For their catalogue send two second class stamps to the above address.*

Index

Other interesting books from Exley Publications:

Help! I've Got a Kid! £7.99 (hardback). Even the best and most caring of parents will find there comes a point when their child becomes a problem and that they are having constant battles over bedtimes, food, fighting with other children or any number of other unpleasant behaviours. This book will help you understand why your child is behaving like this and how to respond positively so that your child is guided into learning good habits. Cleverly illustrated with cartoons to show effective and ineffective approaches to particular problems.

Look, Listen and Play. £7.99 (hardback). A superb new activity book for parents with children aged between three and six. It explores and expands the perceptions of children by making them aware of their five senses and showing them such concepts as big and small, near and far, loud and quiet, or soft and hard. There are dozens of things to do and games to play; most children will find it a source of endless fascination.

Sharing Nature with Children. £5.99 (paperback). A collection of over forty games which children can play in the country, in city parks and in their own gardens. Compiled by a well-known naturalist, Joseph Cornell, these games are great fun. But they also bring a real understanding of such phenomena as camouflage and radar and will widen the children's awareness of the natural world around them.

What It's Like to be Me. £9.99 (paperback). Disabled children from over twenty countries tell other children, parents and teachers what it's really like to be disabled – how they cope, and how they long to be treated just like other children.

'The entries are full of courage and wry humour, and as you might expect, are totally devoid of cloying sentiment ... Very highly recommended ... a valuable contribution towards understanding.' (The Guider).

The Illustrated Address Books series. £5.99 (including VAT, hardback). New from Exley Publications is this superb series of full-colour address books, elegantly bound with picture covers and generous address spaces. Artists featured include Van Gogh, Monet, Breughel, Stubbs, F. Gordon Crosbie and "Spy". The series includes:

The Illustrated Flower Arranging Address Book,
The Illustrated Golf Address Book,
The Illustrated Horse Address Book,
The Illustrated Motoring Address Book,
The Illustrated Wine Address Book.

These books make super presents. Order them from your local bookseller or from Exley Publications Ltd, Dept BP, 16 Chalk Hill, Watford, Herts WD1 4BN. (Please send £1.00 to cover post and packing.) Exley Publications reserves the right to show new retail prices on books which may vary from those previously advertised.